THE
ETERNAL
JOURNEY

THE ETERNAL JOURNEY

How Near-Death Experiences
Illuminate Our Earthly Lives

CRAIG R. LUNDAHL, PH.D., AND
HAROLD A. WIDDISON, PH.D.

WARNER BOOKS

A Time Warner Company

Warner Books, Inc., 1271 Avenue of the Americas, New York, NY 10020
W A Time Warner Company

Printed in the United States of America
First Printing: August 1997
10 9 8 7 6 5 4 3 2 I

Library of Congress Cataloging-in-Publication Data

Lundahl, Craig R.
    The eternal journey : how near-death experiences illuminate our
earthly lives / Craig R. Lundahl and Harold A. Widdison.
        p.   cm.
    Book is based on the author's research of over 200 years of
recorded near-death experiences and from hand-written journals over
100 years old.
    Includes bibliographical references and index.
    ISBN 0-446-52054-3
    I. Future life.   2. Near-death experiences—Religious aspects.
3. Spiritual life.   I. Widdison, Harold A.   II. Title.
BL535.L86   1997
133.9'01'3—dc21   97-12637
                                                              CIP

Book design by Giorgetta B. McRee

As much of heaven is visible as we have eyes to see.

RALPH WALDO EMERSON
American poet (1803–1882)

Dedicated To

Near-death experiencers who shared their glimpses
into eternity so others might know where they came from,
why they are here on earth,
and what awaits them when they die.

Contents

CONTENTS

Acknowledgments

We wish to express our gratitude to our wives, Rafaela Lundahl and Marie Widdison, who contributed to the development of this book by reading the manuscript and providing useful suggestions.

We also want to express our thanks for the enthusiastic support for our book by Warner Books and especially to our editors, Joann Davis and Colleen Kapklein, and their staff for their advice and editorial assistance.

We express our appreciation to Melvin Morse who graciously wrote the foreword for this book.

We also thank Nat Sobel for his assistance in finding a national publisher for this work.

We wish to recognize the pioneer researchers who studied and published near-death experiences many years before the current interest in the subject. Long before Dr. Raymond Moody published his famous book, *Life after Life*, Sir William R. Barrett in 1926 published a fascinating book called *Death-*

Bed Visions. In the early 1960s Dr. Robert Crookall collected thousands of accounts which he published in a number of books. We also acknowledge the work of Duane S. Crowther who compiled a number of Mormon NDEs into a volume published in 1967 under the title of *Life Everlasting.* We also recognize the work of contemporary near-death researchers, many of whom are cited in this book.

We are grateful to Arvin S. Gibson for reviewing the manuscript of this book, for providing us with unpublished materials, and for making many very useful suggestions that we feel strengthened this book.

We gratefully acknowledge the following authors and publishers who granted permissions to use extensively quoted material in this book:

Cedar Fort, Inc., of Springville, Utah, for quotes from Sarah Hinze's *Life Before Life,* Lee Nelson's *Beyond the Veil,* Volume I, and Lee Nelson's *Beyond the Veil,* Volume II.

Chosen Books of Waco, Texas, for quotes from George C. Ritchie and Elizabeth Sherrill's *Return from Tomorrow.*

The Church of Jesus Christ of Latter-Day Saints for quotes from William Dudley Pelley's article "Seven Minutes in Eternity," in *Improvement Era* magazine, John Patterson's article "Was Dead and Came Back to Life Again," in *Millennial Star* magazine, Herr Petersson's article "In the World of Spirits," in *Millennial Star* magazine, and LeRoi Snow's article "Raised from the Dead," in *Improvement Era.*

Duane S. Crowther for quotes from Duane S. Crowther's *Life Everlasting*.

Betty J. Eadie for quotes from Betty J. Eadie and Curtis Taylor's *Embraced by the Light*.

Arvin Gibson for quotes from Arvin S. Gibson's Commentary on "Frightening Near-Death Experiences," in the Winter 1996 *Journal of Near-Death Studies*, Arvin S. Gibson's *Theresa's Story*, and the "Susan Burt" article in the *IANDS of Utah Newsletter* of September–October 1994.

Joseph Heinerman for quotes from Joseph Heinerman's *Guardian Angels*.

Horizon Publishers of Bountiful, Utah, for quotes from Arvin S. Gibson's *Glimpses of Eternity* and Arvin S. Gibson's *Echoes from Eternity*.

The Journal of Death Studies of Bristol, Pennsylvania, for quotes from Michael B. Sabom and Sarah Kreutiziger's article "The Experience of Near-Death."

MBB, Inc., of St. Simons Island, Georgia, for quotes from Raymond Moody's *Reflections on Life after Life*.

Penguin Books of the United Kingdom for quotes from Margot Grey's *Return from Death: An Exploration of the Near-Death Experience*.

Kenneth Ring and Plenum Publishing Corporation of New York for quotes from Kenneth Ring's article "Amazing Grace: The Near-Death Experience as a Compensatory Gift."

William J. Serdahely and Baywood Publishing Company of Amityville, New York, for a quote from William J. Serdahely's article "A Pediatric Near-Death Experience."

William J. Serdahely and Plenum Publishing Corporation of New York for a quote from William J. Serdahely's article "Loving Help from the Other Side: A Mosaic of Some Near-Death, and Near-Death Like, Experiences."

Kevin E. Sorensen for quotes from Michele R. Sorensen and David R. Wilmore's *The Journey beyond Life*, volume I.

The Swedenborg Foundation of New York for a quote from Emanuel Swedenborg's *Heaven and Hell*, translated by George F. Dole, 1990 edition.

Villard Books of New York for quotes from Melvin Morse's *Transformed by the Light*.

We also acknowledge all those other individuals who contributed to this book with their quoted words.

Foreword

by
Melvin Morse, M.D.

Author of *Closer to the Light*, *Transformed by the Light*, and *Parting Visions*

Over a decade ago, Craig Lundahl published the defining scientific analysis of near-death studies of the time. The issues he raised in *A Collection of Near-Death Research Readings* remain to this day the scientific road map for objective research on near-death experiences.

Now, he and coauthor Harold Widdison again present an exhaustive analysis of near-death experiences. After publishing their scientific data in the research literature, they have coauthored a fascinating book. It should be read by anyone interested in what happens to us when we die. For those who believe in life after death, this book will affirm their faith. For those, like me, who can believe only that which is proven, this book will provide the latest scientific evidence and comprehensive case studies necessary for true skeptical inquiry.

For the first time, *The Eternal Journey: How Near-Death Experiences Illuminate Our Earthly Lives* provides an extensive and detailed description of life after death. The authors, drawing on the most extensive historical database of near-death experiences to date, describe the most important purposes of life based on lessons learned from those experiences. In this book, Lundahl and Widdison, two of America's most respected mainstream social scientists, present hundreds of documented near-death experiences. They have distilled from them useful information that has direct practical meaning in our daily lives.

I am amazed and honored that I would be asked to write the foreword for this book. Dr. Lundahl has been one of the most important influences on my own research on near-death experiences. More than any other person, he is responsible for whatever contributions I have made in this field.

I was an arrogant third-year resident in Pediatrics when I heard my first near-death experience. At the time, I thought I already knew all the answers about life and death, and felt that most of those answers could be found in textbooks on critical care medicine. I thought the body was a biological machine. I had the skills to resuscitate dozens of critically ill children from near death, and had seen even more die. I imagined that death was simply the end of life, a smooth transition from unconsciousness to nothingness.

It was only when I took the time to actually listen to my patients who had nearly died that I ultimately came to realize that these experiences teach us what it is like to die, and in turn, how to fully live. The first child who told me of her near-death experience was a Mormon living in Pocatello, Idaho. She was documented as having no heartbeat for nineteen minutes, and when I first attended her, her pupils were fixed and dilated, often a sign of brain death. Yet during this time of profound coma, she perceived herself as being completely aware of her surroundings and accurately described her own resuscitation. She also told me that she perceived herself as going to a place she felt was heaven, meeting religious figures, and returning to life because she wanted to hug her mother again.

When I heard her story I was deeply torn. I absolutely believed that she believed her story, and was struck by the many tiny details of her own resuscitation that she accurately described. I felt positive that through unknown neurological mechanisms, she somehow was awake and having an extraordinary spiritual journey during the time I knew she was comatose and dying.

Yet my scientific training dismissed the experience as fantasy or hallucination. I am not religious in any way and spend little time pondering philosophical or spiritual issues. I am far more comfortable intubating children or inserting threadlike catheters into their arteries than discussing the spiritual implications of visions they might be having while we are performing those very same procedures. My fellow physicians at Seattle Children's Hospital and I felt that certainly these experiences were some sort of artifact of resuscitation, perhaps caused by hallothane, an anesthetic agent.

At that time, the level of research in near-death studies was very low, and rarely in mainstream medical journals. Most of it was the level of anecdote or simple storytelling. The leading experts on death and dying considered near-death research to be little more than campfire stories.

Another emotional hurdle for me was that I had little in common with the leading near-death researchers. My main research interests were the effects of radiation and anticancer drugs on the brain. I was a rat brain surgeon by day and worked for Air Lift Northwest as a flight physician at night. As a medical scientist, I was unfamiliar with most of the journals in the field and had a hard time even getting them. At the time I was in training to be a Pediatric Neurologist and did not see anything of scientific merit in studying the spiritual visions of the dying.

Reading Dr. Lundahl's first book changed all that for me. For the first time, I had a scientific framework to use to research near-death experiences. I realized to my great surprise that near-death experiences were not simply some sort of New Age fad, but had been the subject of serious scrutiny from the scientific mainstream. Realizing that someone of Craig Lundahl's credentials and scientific stature was involved in near-death research gave me courage in designing my own research project and defending it to the harsh scrutiny of my hospital's Human Subject Review Board.

My first study of childhood near-death experiences was directly based on Dr. Widdison's chapter in that book. Dr. Widdison pointed out that science must be totally objective and be willing to entertain any hypothesis capable of explaining observed facts. Suddenly I realized that my assumption that the body was a biological machine was just as speculative as the belief in life after death. After reading the entire book, which spanned the entire range of studies and theories about near-death experiences, I became for the first time, a true skeptic about near-death experiences.

After reading Dr. Lundahl's first book, I felt directly challenged to attempt to prove my assumption that near-death experiences were simply a result of the brain attempting to deal with lack of oxygen, stress, medications, and cultural assumptions about death. I was astonished that mainstream social scientists with impeccable credentials were using the case material of near-death experiences to challenge our prevailing scientific assumptions. Most mainstream social sciences have no need of the hypothesis that there is a god or soul to man to explain human behavior.

Yet after over one hundred years of our intellectual establishment embracing scientific materialism, if these authors were correct, we are clearly on the verge of a major paradigm shift in our understanding of reality. As my research team at Seattle Children's Hospital discussed this, we realized that a similar revolution was going on in the so-called hard sciences of physics and mathematics. Scientists in those fields were discovering mystical insights similar to those found in near-death experiences. These scientists were discovering the same mystical insights into life I heard from children, but from the perspective of the new sciences of quantum physics and chaos mathematical theory.

Our first study documented, to our great surprise, that these experiences are not the result of medications, psychological stress, or a lack of oxygen to the brain, but somehow integral to the processes of dying. Our research was strong enough to be published in the American Medical Association's *Pediatric Journal.* It has subsequently been replicated by other studies, including experimental laboratory research done at the National Warfare Institute. After rigorous and intense scientific scrutiny, it is now generally accepted that near-death experiences represent the only objective evidence of what it is like to die.

There is and should be a higher scientific standard for research which contradicts the prevailing scientific theories of a given era. New ideas must stand the inferno of peer review to separate out the junk science and pseudoscience. We know that we only know a fraction of what is to be known, and yet, to consider new thoughts means giving up the comfortable old ones. So it is proper that we demand to inspect the credentials and methods of the researchers and rigorously review for ourselves the raw data upon which conclusions are drawn.

Drs. Lundahl and Widdison are scientists of the highest caliber. The field of near-death studies could never have been taken seriously enough to spawn the sort of research I and my colleagues have done without the prestige they have imparted. Dr. Lundahl and Dr. Widdison have long and distinguished academic careers, earning the respect of their colleagues primarily for research and teaching outside the field of near-death studies.

Dr. Lundahl is chairman emeritus of the Department of Social Sciences and Professor Emeritus at Western New Mexico University. He is the recipient of numerous major grants in diverse areas such as juvenile justice, housing, solar energy, and community outreach teaching programs. He has numerous awards and honors from virtually every professional organization he is involved with.

Dr. Widdison has a degree in industrial management and worked for five years for the United States Atomic Energy Commission. He is a full professor at Northern Arizona University, and has been an acknowledged expert on death and dying for twenty-five years. His degree is in medical sociology from Case Western Reserve University.

Now, for the first time, these scientists leave the ivory tower and present their findings for the general public. *The Eternal Journey* is based on the authors' research of over two hundred years of recorded near-death experiences with some from the

Mormon community. Mormons have a long tradition of carefully documenting deathbed visions and near-death experiences. Many of the experiences the authors present are taken directly from hand-written journals over one hundred years old. These experiences are an amazing treasure trove of spiritual information, as they were recorded long before our current understanding and mass public awareness of the phenomenon.

One of the difficult issues in near-death research is separating out the core dying experience from cultural perceptions of what should be happening at death. Our current cultural preoccupation with near-death experiences is so pervasive, that even children's videos such as "All Dogs Go to Heaven," have images of going to heaven through a tunnel. The rich case histories presented in this book represent an invaluable cross cultural contribution to the scientific literature. Many of these experiences were documented long before there were radio and television talk shows. We have a lot to learn from studying them.

It is rare to read a book which is based on serious scientific research and yet has the emotional impact to become a popular best seller. The case histories are required reading for any serious student of near-death studies. For example, recently Chilean neuroscientist Juan Gomez Jeria called for a book to be published with the sort of information found in *The Eternal Journey*, stating "this information would clearly help us to construct scientific models to explain near-death experiences."

This book is easy to read. The authors move effortlessly from story to story. Their message is clear and inspiring. I greatly admire this book's ability to discuss profound and complex scientific concepts with grace and clarity. Any person can learn from and be inspired by this book. The unique contribution of this book is that it summarizes many hundreds of books, articles, and accounts into an integrated whole.

This book is more than fascinating case histories. It is the wisdom that the authors have learned from studying them, wisdom they share with us in this wonderful book. This is the sort of book people read over and over again, understanding something different each time. It is the sort of book that people buy ten copies of for all their friends and family. *The Eternal Journey* will make you laugh, make you cry, and teach you something about how to live a more joyous life.

CHAPTER 1

Introduction

What is the purpose of life and the meaning of death? Since the dawn of human history the mystery of the meaning and purpose of life and death has engaged the human imagination. It is now possible to address these most important questions by examining carefully findings from the scientific study of persons who have experienced death and returned to life with the knowledge of the real purpose of life and an understanding of the nature and purpose of death. This information resulted in a new scientific field, the field of near-death studies.

Scientific research on the phenomenon that has become labeled as the "near-death experience," or NDE, is now in its third decade. This research was initiated in 1975 with the publication of the best-selling book *Life after Life*, by the psychiatrist Raymond A. Moody Jr. Moody's book was based on his research of the near-death cases of 150 persons. They had experienced an apparent clinical death or a very close brush with death during an accident, severe injury, or illness. This classic work soon became well-known not only to the general public, but also to the scientific community. It was soon followed by the near-death research projects of Kenneth Ring, Michael Sabom, John Audette, Ian Stevenson, Bruce Greyson, Craig Lundahl, Fred Schoonmaker, and George Gallup Jr.

The Traits of the Near-Death Experience

From his analysis of 150 near-death cases, Dr. Moody developed a list of the most common elements of the near-death experience. These common elements are (1) a sense of ineffability, (2) hearing the news, (3) feelings of peace or quiet, (4) a noise, (5) the dark tunnel, (6) leaving the physical body, (7) meeting others, (8) a being of light, (9) the review, (10) the border, and (11) coming back.

The first element, "ineffability," referred to the fact that persons who had an NDE report it is difficult to express the experience in words because ordinary language is inadequate for describing what they have undergone. Persons who have NDEs also say they "hear the news" when their doctors or others pronounce them dead. Many of the NDErs report a third element—that of experiencing or "feeling extreme peace." In many cases NDErs report various auditory sensations such as a buzzing noise or heavenly sounds at or near death. Often NDErs report a fifth element, the sensation of being pulled very rapidly through some kind of dark space like a "dark tunnel." A sixth element is a movement "out of the body." At this point, the NDEr is outside his or her body and, in many cases, looking down and seeing his or her own physical body from some point outside it. At some point while near death, NDErs may experience a seventh element when they meet other spiritual beings, usually deceased loved ones. Probably one of the most dramatic elements in reports of NDEs is an encounter with a being emanating a very bright light. Moody found this eighth element, "the being of light," to be the most incredible common element in the NDE accounts he studied. It is also the element that has the most profound effect upon the NDEr. All the NDErs who experienced a being of light in Moody's study say that it is not only a being of light, but a personal being who emanates indescribable love and warmth. The ninth element in the NDE is "the review," a rapid panoramic review of the NDEr's life. A tenth element is experiencing a border or limit of some kind beyond which the NDEr cannot pass. At some point during the NDE, the NDEr is told to make a decision to come back to his or her physical body, or returns to it automatically.

In 1977 Moody described four less common events or elements that generally occurred during NDEs of longer duration. These elements are (1) vision of knowledge, (2) cities of light, (3) a realm of bewildered spirits, and (4) supernatural rescues. The element "vision of knowledge" refers to the NDEr experiencing a feeling of complete knowledge. NDErs also report catching a glimpse of another realm usually termed "heavenly" with cities and physical structures. This realm Moody refers to as "cities of light." Another element, "a realm of bewildered spirits," is reported by NDErs who had glimpses of other beings who seemed trapped in a miserable state of existence. Finally, some NDErs said they were saved from physical death by the interposition of a spiritual being or experienced "supernatural rescues."

3

In 1988 Moody refined his list of elements to nine traits that NDErs may experience. The traits include a sense of being dead, peace and painlessness even during a "painful" experience, bodily separation, entering a dark region or tunnel, rising rapidly into the heavens, meeting deceased friends and relatives who are bathed in light, encountering a Supreme Being, reviewing one's life, and feeling reluctance to return to the world of the living.

Research on the Near-Death Experience

Other research on the NDE soon followed Moody's original work. In 1978 Maurice Rawlings, a cardiologist, reported that 20 percent of the patients he resuscitated describe NDEs; he also reported some hellish NDEs. The cardiologist Michael B. Sabom and Sarah Kreutiziger found 61 NDEs in 100 patients who had been unconscious and near death. In 1979 the sociologist Craig R. Lundahl examined 11 accounts of Mormon NDEs, 9 of them occurring before 1923. The psychologist Kenneth Ring surveyed 102 near-death survivors, and half of them reported experiences containing NDE elements. His data suggested that the "core" experience consisted of five distinct stages: peace, body separation, entering the darkness, seeing the light, and entering the light. He also surveyed 17 suicide survivors in 1982 who reported they experienced all of the various elements commonly found in accounts of NDEs. The researchers James H. Lindley, Sethyn Bryan, and Bob Conley analyzed 49 NDErs in the Pacific Northwest of the United States in 1981. George Gallup Jr., the pollster, found in a national survey of NDEs published in

1990 that 22 million people reported having a near-death experience. Paola Giovetti studied 120 Italian accounts of NDEs and other deathbed phenomena. In 1983 Nancy E. Bush, a prominent NDE researcher and NDEr, reported that the experiences most often found in 17 accounts of children are comparable in content with those reported by adults. Timothy J. Green and Penelope Friedman studied 50 NDEs in a Southern California population. Margot Grey assessed the reports of 32 English and 9 American NDEs in 1985. The medical doctor Melvin Morse reported on 7 childhood NDEs in 1986. The nuclear engineer Arvin Gibson reported on 68 NDErs in the Salt Lake City, Utah, region in 1994, and P. H. M. Atwater has interviewed over 2,000 cases since 1985.

Studies examining NDEs in various geographical and demographical populations throughout the world as well as in special populations and reports of individual cases continue to this day and can be expected to continue into the foreseeable future.

From the research in near-death studies, the NDE has been established as a certifiable phenomenon that occurs to many people who come close to clinical death or experience it. This brief survey of these major research findings also suggests that the NDE is a pervasive phenomenon occurring across time, cultures, and ages and that it continues to have many common characteristics.

The Near-Death Experience Process

Research in the field of near-death studies shows there are three major modes of near-death onset—a serious illness, a major accident, or a suicide attempt—that may bring people close to death. Only when a person is near death can he or she have an NDE. According to the national survey conducted by George Gallup Jr. in 1981, about 35 percent of all people who have a verge-of-death or temporary death experience have an NDE.

We now know that demographic variables such as age, sex, race, social class, educational level, income, occupation, religious affiliation, size of city or town, region of residence, and marital status do not significantly influence the incidence or contents of NDEs. Personal factors or prior knowledge of NDEs does not have any effect on NDEs, either. However, prolonged unconsciousness does affect NDE incidence and depth. Research also shows NDE incidence as well as depth is greatest for illness victims, moderate for accident victims, and weakest for those who attempt suicide.

An NDE usually begins with a feeling of peace and/or well-being, as well as with a loss of pain. Sixty percent of the subjects in Ring's study experienced a peace stage, and 100 percent of the subjects in the study by Sabom experienced peace. Seventy-four percent of the subjects in the Evergreen Study conducted by Lindley, Bryan, and Conley, 70 percent in Green and Friedman's study, and 46 percent in Gibson's study reported a sense of peace. Gallup found that 32 percent of a national sample experienced a sense of peace.

Of course, efforts to resuscitate the NDEr may conclude the NDE. Probably because of current medical technology that allows quick resuscitation of patients, many NDEs do not develop to deeper levels. It is also probably true that current medical technology allows many persons to experience an NDE and return to tell about it who otherwise would not.

As the NDE continues, research generally suggests the next phase is a separation from the physical body. Ring's study showed that 37 percent of NDErs experience the body separation stage, while 100 percent of Sabom's subjects, 71 percent of the Evergreen Study's subjects, 66 percent of Green and Friedman's subjects, and 86 percent of Gibson's subjects had this experience. Twenty-six percent of Gallup's national sample had an out-of-body sensation. Generally, once NDErs see and recognize their physical bodies after leaving the body, they sense being dead.

Research findings indicate they may next enter a darkness: a dark tunnel or a void. Twenty-three percent of Ring's subjects experienced entering the darkness stage or a darkness, as did 23 percent of Sabom's subjects, 38 percent of the Evergreen Study subjects, 32 percent of Green and Friedman's subjects, and 22 percent of Gibson's subjects. Gallup found 9 percent of his national sample experienced the tunnel.

This phase of the NDE is followed by seeing the light. Sixteen percent of Ring's subjects reported seeing the light. Twenty-eight percent of Sabom's subjects, 56 percent of the Evergreen Study's subjects, 62 percent of Green and Friedman's subjects, and 60 percent of Gibson's subjects saw it, too. Fourteen percent of Gallup's national sample saw the light. Ring found in his study that suicide NDEs never reached the seeing the light and entering the light stages, while the NDEr who undergoes a serious illness is more likely to experience these stages.

As the NDE continues to the deepest level, the NDEr is likely to enter another world and encounter a being of light, a presence, and/or meet others. Ten percent of Ring's subjects, 54 percent of Sabom's subjects, 32 percent of Gallup's national sample, 39 percent of the subjects in the Evergreen Study, and 18 percent of Green and Friedman's subjects entered another realm or world. Twenty-two percent of Gibson's subjects saw some type of landscape feature, and 7 percent saw buildings. Once NDErs are in this new environment they usually meet a being of light, a presence, or others. Sabom reported that 48 percent of his subjects reported meeting others, Gallup reported 23 percent of his national sample reported the presence of a special being or beings, and 55 percent of Gibson's subjects encountered others. If the NDEr meets a presence or a being of light, he or she will probably experience a life review. In his national sample, Gallup found that 32 percent of the NDErs experienced a life review. Sabom found that 3 percent of his subjects had a life review, and in his study, Gibson found that 11 percent of his subjects had a life review.

At any time during the NDE, the NDE may be terminated because of an alternative to death, namely, an opportunity to return to life. This often happens when the NDEr is asked if he or she would like to return to life following the life review but may occur at any time during an NDE.

Once the NDEr has encountered a presence, a being of light, or other people or undergone a life review, he or she is asked to decide whether to return to life or told they must return to life. It is very likely that when the NDEr is given the option of returning to life, he or she will decide to return to the body or, if reluctant to do so, is soon persuaded to do so.

It is a certainty that when an NDEr is told to return to life, the NDEr does it.

An Ideal Description of a Near-Death Experience

To provide a better understanding of the NDE process, let us consider a brief "ideal" description of an NDE. This brief "ideal" experience embodies all the common elements in the order in which it is typical for them to occur. However, they normally do not all occur in any actual NDE, nor do they appear in an invariant sequence.

Jane is seriously ill from kidney failure and multiple associated complications and is dying from her illness. As she reaches the greatest distress her heart stops, she quits breathing, and she loses consciousness.

She begins to feel a sense of peace and well-being. She notices that she no longer has pain. Suddenly she finds herself separated from her body and in the air above her physical body, looking down at it, where she sees a physician and two nurses working to resuscitate her. At this point she begins to realize she is dead, but she still has a body, acute vision and hearing, and a clear and alert mental state.

After ten minutes she still remains physically unconscious as she hears herself pronounced dead. Then she enters a dark space. At the end of this dark space, she sees a brilliant light, and upon entering this light, she finds herself in another world of preternatural beauty.

She now meets the Being of Light who takes her through a life review and helps her put all the events of her life in perspective. The life review takes place in what seems like an instant, and is a full-color, three-dimensional, panoramic review of everything Jane has done in her life. She perceives the effects of all her actions upon the people in her life. She also feels all her emotions as well as those of the people in her life review. It is much as if she is reliving her life.

At any time during the NDE, the NDE may be terminated because of an alternative to death, namely, an option to return to life. This often happens when the NDEr is asked if he or she would like to return to life. However, Jane, who has been suffering from a serious illness, continues her deep NDE.

Eventually, though, Jane is asked by the Being of Light if she wants to return to life, and she begins to contemplate her responsibilities to her family. Although she is reluctant to go back, she finally decides to do so. When her spirit reenters the body, the former pain and suffering returns. She eventually recovers from her illness, and as a result of her NDE she loses all fear of death and experiences a change in her values, attitudes, and behaviors.

This NDE description could just as easily show Jane meeting her deceased relatives in the otherworld, who tell her that she will have to return to life because it is not her time yet. Under these circumstances, Jane may not have experienced a life review.

Purposes of the Book

This book is a careful analysis of the experiences of hundreds of reliable individuals who have died and then returned to life to tell about it. To most of these individuals, the experience bordered on the sacred and altered their lives permanently. Most participants share their experiences reluctantly, and when they do, it is out of a desire to help others appreciate life, to understand who they are and to testify that death is not the end of all.

The book presents experience after experience from NDErs that can enlighten us about the reality, purposes, and meaning of life and death. We should acquire a new understanding of life based on these experiences. This increased understanding should leave all of us with a new view of death and a motivation to live better lives.

Kenneth Ring said that not everyone needs to have an NDE, but they can incorporate lessons learned from the NDE into their own lives.

Speaking of learning from other people's near-death experiences, Melvin Morse writes:

> So what? say the skeptics. So what if near-death experiencers don't have a fear of death like the rest of us? So what if they are zestful about life? So what if they are less likely to have deep depressions and feelings of futility that lead to suicide? So what? What does that have to do with the rest of us?
>
> The answer is simple: Learn what you can about life from these brushes with death, even if they are the experiences of other people.

So as Morse goes on to say, "The key is to listen. By listening to the dying themselves, we can learn to understand many mysteries of life and death."

Morse further states that "so many of society's problems—drug addiction, depression, the chaos and despair of inner cities, and the environmental disasters we are inflicting upon ourselves—speak to a lack of understanding that all of life is interconnected and with purpose."

Plan of the Book

In the introduction of this book we discussed the scientific study being done in the field of near-death studies of persons who have had a near-death experience or NDE and returned to life to tell about it. The elements in the NDE identified through research and a detailed description and illustration of the NDE process were given. We addressed the major reason for this book, which is to answer the questions we began with in this chapter: "What is the purpose of life and the meaning of death?"

Following this introduction to the field of near-death studies, chapter 2 shows how prevalent the NDE is in society. It also gives evidence for the reality of the NDE and that it is a certifiable phenomenon occurring to many people who come close to clinical death or experience it.

The pre-earth life is the subject of chapter 3. Chapter 3 is concerned with some fascinating and newly published findings on a pre-earth life and its activities and purposes. For the information in this chapter, heavy reliance will be placed upon NDE cases where NDErs saw the pre-mortal world or remembered it and NDE cases of unborn children.

Chapter 4 examines earth life and the purposes of earth life, and chapter 5 describes how death is a transition from earth life into a post-earth life. These chapters are based on published NDEs that are used for illustrative purposes.

The subject of the final part of the book, chapters 6 through 14, is the post-earth life. This section of the book will present near-death research findings on the post-earth life. Chapter 6 describes the meaning and experience of death. The nature of the spirit body that survives death is described in chapter 7. The location of the world of light as revealed by children, by the dying, and by near-death accounts is the subject of chapter 8. In chapter 9, areas surrounding the City of Light are described, and the City of Light itself is described in chapter 10. The life found in the City of Light is described in chapter 11. Chapter 12 looks at the purposes of post-earth life. In chapter 13, the appearance and activities of those described as angels is presented. Chapter 14 describes the realm of bewildered spirits found in the otherworld. The contents of all these chapters will be based primarily on the experiences of those who have journeyed to this otherworld. Throughout these chapters the authors quote extensively from published NDEs for illustrative purposes.

The interconnectedness of the pre-earth life, earth life, and the post-earth life is explored in chapter 15.

In the concluding chapter of this book, chapter 16, there will be a brief discussion of the significance of the findings in the book for humanity and the individual.

CHAPTER 2

The Reality of the Near-Death Experience

How prevalent are near-death experiences? Today, thousands of persons who have had NDEs have been interviewed by near-death researchers. Raymond Moody alone has interviewed more than a thousand NDErs.

The landmark study carried out in 1980–81 by the prestigious Gallup Poll organization and reported by George Gallup Jr. in the book *Adventures in Immortality* found that eight million adults in the United States have had an NDE. He did a follow up study in 1990 and discovered that the figure had increased to over 22 million. That means one person in every eleven in the United States has had an NDE. Furthermore, Gallup's findings also suggest that approximately 35 percent of those persons who have come close to death undergo an NDE.

What do these figures mean? Without question, we are dealing with a widespread phenomenon.

The Reality of the NDE

Is the NDE a real event, and what evidence is there to support this assertion? You have thousands of persons who claim to have had NDEs who have been interviewed by near-death researchers, as well as millions of Americans who report having had an NDE. In addition, further evidence is found in historical NDEs, in Michael B. Sabom's hospital room experiment, in child NDEs, in the aftereffects on individuals of their experience, in NDE flashforwards, and in the lack of suitable alternative explanations for the NDE.

Interviews. After thousands of interviews, near-death researchers have come to a realization that all these NDErs cannot be fabricating fiction. NDErs report them with such deep sincerity that it seems unlikely they are making them up. Also, there are simply too many parallels and too many common elements from one case to the next. The accumulated interviews in the field over almost twenty years involving many studies fail to show contradictions. Rather, they tend to show confirmation of the NDE as an authentic phenomenon.

Historical NDEs. Near-death experiences are not new to this era of time. Rather, they have spanned many centuries. They have been described or recorded in ancient writings such as *The Egyptian Book of the Dead, The Tibetan Book of the Dead*, Plato's *Republic*, the Old and New Testament of the Bible, and *The Aztec Song of the Dead* and in historical publications such as *Dialogues* by Gregory the Great and Emanuel Swedenborg's *Heaven and Hell*. Numerous NDE accounts exist in the literature published in the past three hundred years. At the end of

15

the nineteenth century scientists in England and America were investigating the growing number of accounts involving deathbed and near-death visions. Even a religious group in the United States, known today as the Church of Jesus Christ of Latter-day Saints, had information on the NDE as early as the 1830s. In the 1950s a number of prominent individuals had NDEs, such as the writer Ernest Hemingway, the explorer Richard Byrd, and the psychologist Carl Jung. In summary, NDEs have been described and recorded for many years and across many cultures, but only lately has rigorous scientific analysis been applied to study them.

Sabom's Experiment. Many anecdotal NDE cases exist in which the reality of the out-of-body element can be independently verified by external conditions, situations, people, and objects. One such well-known case was reported by Professor Kimberly Clark of the University of Washington, Seattle, concerning a patient named Maria who suffered a cardiac arrest. Maria described an out-of-body experience during her NDE and saw a tennis shoe on an outside ledge of the hospital as she floated out of the hospital. During her recovery Maria described her NDE to Professor Clark and told her what she had seen. She asked Professor Clark to search for the tennis shoe to assure herself that she had really seen it. So Professor Clark went outside and looked up at the ledges for the tennis shoe but could not see one.

This is what Professor Clark said about this event:

> Finally, I found a room where I pressed my face
> to the glass and saw the tennis shoe! My vantage

point was very different from what Maria's had to have been for her to notice that the little toe had worn a place in the shoe and that the lace was stuck under the heel and other details about the side of the shoe not visible to me. The only way she would have had such a perspective was if she had been floating right outside and at very close range to the tennis shoe.

She retrieved the shoe and took it back to Maria. This incident was very concrete evidence for Professor Clark of the reality of NDEs.

Another such case was that of Susan Burt, who had an NDE after a heart attack following the birth of her twins in 1992. Susan had been wondering about her NDE and wanted to verify that some of the things she saw during her medical emergency were also seen by others. So she contacted the anesthesiologist and arranged to meet with him. She described to him the details of what she saw while she was out of her body watching the doctors and nurses work on her. He confirmed her version of the events and told her that the medical team later changed their procedures so that they could be better prepared to meet similar emergencies in the future.

One effort to test the out-of-body element of the NDE experimentally was that of the cardiologist Michael B. Sabom. He presented several cases of NDErs who saw the details of the hospital room while out of their bodies. Sabom was able to interview members of the medical teams, to talk with family members who had pertinent information, and to use medical records in each of these cases. Then he matched the patients' descriptions of the situations with the actual situations as reconstructed from the known facts in each case. Sabom found that the patients (NDErs) accurately described the details of the hospital room, which they could not have seen given the location of their bodies, nor would they have known because of their physical condition. There are also many other similar opportunities for partial corroboration of NDEs besides Sabom's experiment that have been cited in the literature. That these NDErs in Sabom's experiment had accurate perceptions of occurrences in the hospital room while experiencing a near-death crisis event lends further credence to the reality of the NDE.

Child NDEs. The NDEs of children are important additional evidence of the reality of the NDE. These cases are very special because near-death researchers are studying persons who are relatively free of cultural conditioning and have no prior knowledge of the NDE. Several researchers have investigated child NDEs, and the findings of this research show that children report the same events in their experiences as do adults, except they do not experience the equivalent of a life review, and many more of them see the Being of Light.

NDE Aftereffects. The NDE transforms the people who have them. Researchers have observed the effects of the NDE on the lives of NDErs and found that NDErs outwardly show measurable changes in attitude and behavior toward life that are attributable only to the NDE.

In his original study, Raymond Moody reported that NDErs felt their NDEs broadened and deepened their lives, caused them to become more reflective and more concerned with philosophical issues, changed their attitude toward physical life, changed their concepts of the mind and its importance, taught them the importance of cultivating love for others, taught them the importance of seeking knowledge, and changed their attitude toward physical death.

In his systematic study on the NDE, Kenneth Ring found that the typical near-death survivor emerges from the NDE with a heightened sense of appreciation for life and a determination to live life to the fullest, with a renewed sense of purpose in living, and as a stronger person who values love and service to others and no longer feels that material comforts in life are so important. Ring also found that NDErs who report a "core" experience experienced a heightened spiritual awareness, feared death less or lost their fear of death, and believed more definitely in an afterlife following their NDEs.

Sabom found that almost all subjects interviewed in his study viewed their NDE as an important event that had done more to shape their life goals and attitudes than any other previous experience. Sabom found NDErs' death anxiety was dramatically reduced or eliminated by their NDEs. They developed a new fervor for day-to-day living and a new attitude toward death. Their religious views were commonly strengthened by the NDE, but not necessarily their religious involvement in a church. They also developed a new personal interest in the caring and loving aspects of human relationships.

Gallup reported a variety of NDE aftereffects from his nationwide survey of NDEs in America. Among these aftereffects are a lessening of the fear of death, a strengthening of personal religious beliefs, a heightened perception of life's brevity and a determination to live every moment intensely, a lessening of intimidation by the demands of life, an increased concern about fellow men and women, an increased sensitivity to one's place in the world, a feeling of increased control over life, and a willingness to sacrifice for others.

Other research on the aftereffects of the NDE in the 1980s supported the findings of Moody, Ring, Sabom, and Gallup. Since 1982 interest in the aftereffects of the NDE has continued with publications by many NDE researchers. Here are just a few of these studies and their major findings.

Timothy Green and Penelope Friedman reported their subjects felt definite changes in values away from materialistic and toward spiritual goals. Their subjects appeared to be more loving and more aware of their relationships with others. They were more conscious of the meaning and purpose of their lives. Their subjects reported less fear of death or no fear at all and an unshakable conviction that they will exist following physical death.

Cherie Sutherland's Australian study of 50 NDErs found a significant shift away from organized religion and church attendance and toward private informal prayer and meditation, a belief in life after death, a lack of fear of death, and an attitude against attempting suicide. When Sutherland asked the NDErs the most significant change to come about as a result of their NDEs, spiritual growth, a loving attitude, knowing God, and inner peace were mentioned as the most meaningful changes by the majority of the NDErs.

Melvin Morse, who studied the NDEs of children, found many have no fear of death as a result of their NDEs. One child became very religious, while another said you can be with God without the rules of religion. Children who had NDEs also felt that life is precious and that there is a purpose in life. Morse reports that one child spoke frequently in grade school about the need to love one another after his NDE. Other children, following their NDEs, mention the importance of acquiring knowledge, that little in life is worth getting upset over, and to be more tolerant of other people's beliefs.

P. H. M. Atwater's research shows that the transformation resulting from NDEs can and does have long-term negative consequences that plague many near-death survivors the rest of their lives. Examples are that displays of an unconditional love toward everybody by the NDEr after the NDE put a particular strain on relationships with family members, and they become very vulnerable to exploitation by unscrupulous people because they are so trusting following the NDE. Atwater has found that NDErs are changed so significantly that they are no longer the person they were before their experience. These transformations can cause serious complications for family, friends, and employers.

A review of these studies shows they are consistent in their findings about the aftereffects of the NDE and the NDEr. In other words, the NDE effects changes in the values, attitudes, and behavior of the NDEr. They seem to cause total changes in personalities. As Moody said, "That NDEs totally transform the people to whom they happen shows their reality and power."

NDE Flashforwards. In 1980 Kenneth Ring coined the term "flashforwards" to refer to the phenomena where some NDErs were permitted to see their future life on earth during their life review.

As stated earlier, the life review is one of the elements of the NDE where the NDEr experiences a panoramic life review in which, typically, the NDEr reports seeing an extremely vivid, real, and extraordinarily rapid display of visual imagery depicting various events of his or her life extending to very early childhood.

To illustrate a flashforward, Ring briefly recounted a case of a woman who had an NDE in 1972 while recovering from surgery:

> At one point during her NDE, she found herself facing what she described as an "enormous television screen." On the screen she was shown—in vivid color—various scenes from her life in a very rapid sequence of realistic images. Following that display, the screen disappeared but was followed by a second screen. That one, however, was dark and the images—in black and white this time—were much murkier and more difficult to discern. Nevertheless, she remembers being shown, among other events, the deaths of two members of her family (who were not ill at the time of this woman's NDE) and told that she would play a special role in caring for these persons during their terminal illnesses. This NDEr has averred to me that these events, apparently disclosed during her flashforwards, did indeed come to pass.

In Gallup's 1982 nationwide survey of Americans, he found approximately a half million adult Americans out of eight million of those who have had an NDE had a premonition about some event or events that would happen in the future during their NDE. For example, some of the people in the Gallup study reported "that during near-death encounters or other related experiences, they learned of events that were in the process of happening at some distance or would happen in the future."

Similar to flashforwards is what Craig Lundahl labeled "otherworld personal future revelations." Otherworld personal future revelations (OPFRs) are very similar to flashforwards in that they are a preview of a personal event or events that will occur in the NDEr's future life on earth but differ mainly from flashforwards in that a future personal event or events is told to the NDEr during a visit to the otherworld by deceased relatives, deceased friends, or by an escort.

To illustrate an otherworld personal future revelation, Lundahl cited the case of Walter P. Monson, who had an NDE in 1923. Monson was apparently in the otherworld for only a few moments and then returned to mortality. He gave this account:

> One evening just before Christmas while addressing an audience at the old Farmers' Ward chapel on South State Street, I was stricken with intense pain from a strangulated hernia. That night I underwent an abdominal operation. My condition was so serious and my chances of living so slight that the doctors did not remove the afflicted section. They simply sewed up the wound, feeling that it was only a matter of a few hours at most before I would die.
>
> Next morning when I awoke my family and others were kneeling about my bed and Bishop

LeGrand Richards of the Sugarhouse Ward was praying for my recovery.

At midnight I was fully awake. I heard the Christmas chimes and felt the nurse taking my pulse and temperature. Suddenly, a coldness attacked my feet and hands. It moved up my limbs and up my arms towards my body. I felt it reach my heart. There was a slight murmur. I gasped for breath and lapsed into unconsciousness, so far as all things mortal.

As I turned my head in the direction I intended to go, I saw my little daughter, Elna, who had died twenty-one years before. She was more mature than when she passed away, and was most beautiful to my eyes, so full of life, intelligence, and sweetness. As she came towards me she raised her right hand and said, "Go back, Papa, I want Richard first. Then Grandma must come, and then Mama is coming, before you."

The next thing I knew was my body gasping for breath. I felt my heart action start and was conscious of the coldness leaving my body. All numbness left me and the natural warmth returned. I felt the nurse shaking me and heard her say, "Mr. Monson, you must not let yourself slip like that again."

Monson left the following account of the passing of the others of his family as foretold in his NDE:

For five weeks I remained in the hospital, gaining a little strength each day. . . . Mrs. Monson vis-

24

ited me every day with my son Richard. She was told by the doctor, C. F. Wilcox, that there was no hope for my recovery, and of course, her visits were attended with deep emotion.

Many times little Richard, for he was barely six years old, took my hand and pressed it affectionately against his cheek. "Daddy," he would say anxiously, "you're not going to die, are you?" I could not control my emotions, try as I would, but I managed to say, "No, Dick, it is not my turn."

Four weeks after I returned home, my boy, Richard passed away. During the last hours of his life he sat up in bed, opened his big blue eyes, and looked toward the door with intense interest. "Come in, Elna," he said, "there's only Papa and Mama here."

I asked him whom he could see and he answered, "Elna is there. It's funny you can't see her. And there are a whole lot of people with her who want me to come."

He called his mother to the bed and put his arms around her neck. "Can I go with Elna?" he asked.

"Yes, my dear," she answered. "You have suffered enough."

"Then I'll go. And I'll be happy if you will promise not to cry once for me," he pleaded.

Mrs. Monson gave him the promise he wished and left the room.

"Daddy," he said to me, "come here. I guess Mama has gone out to cry."

He paused a moment, then turned and looked in the direction of the door and listened intently at something he evidently heard.

"Dear old Daddy," he went on at length, "so you promised at the hospital I could go. Now I know why you cried when I said, 'You are not going to die, are you, daddy?'"

Three hours later his eyes closed in eternal sleep.

How he knew that I wept because I had been told by Elna that he was to go first and that my coming back was equivalent to a promise that he might precede me to the great beyond, can only be explained through knowledge given him from Elna herself, for he knew nothing of the circumstance of what I saw and heard while my spirit was separated from my body at the hospital.

Three weeks after his passing, I visited my mother, Ellen Monson, at Preston, Idaho. Mother had been a sufferer for many years, but her constitution was strong and the doctor had told her that she had every chance of living for ten or fifteen years. She lamented the fact that she was spared, while my boy was taken. She said she had desired to die for twenty-two years. Without realizing what I said, I made her this promise: "Mother, you haven't twenty-two days to suffer."

Nineteen days from that time, mother left us. And six years from the time of mother's death, Mrs. Monson passed away.

Other researchers have reported flashforwards, too. Although the number of flashforwards is relatively small and they have not been widely researched, their verification is further evidence of the reality of the NDE.

No Alternative Explanations for the NDE. There have been many attempts to explain NDEs as physical or mental phenomena. These attempts fall into a number of categories of explanation that include pharmacological, physiological, neurological, psychological, cultural, and religious.

Moody, Morse, Ring, Sabom, and Karlis Osis and Erlendur Haraldsson have each studied these explanations carefully. They examined pharmacological factors such as therapeutic drugs as a possible explanation of the NDE and found they do not explain the NDE. There have also been attempts to explain NDEs as due to a lack of oxygen to the brain or some other type of severe bodily stress. However, the empirical evidence tends to undermine these physiological explanations. They examined neurological explanations such as temporal lobe seizures and found these explanations do not fit the NDE. Hallucinations, visions, dreams, depersonalization, memories of birth, wishful thinking, psychological expectations, or psychic phenomena have been used in psychological attempts to explain the NDE. Moody, Ring, Sabom, and Morse found that these psychological explanations are not identical to NDEs. Studies, particularly studies by Ring and Morse, have shown that cultural and religious explanations also fail to explain the NDE. To be valid, an explanation or theory for the NDE must be able to explain all NDEs fully, not just some NDEs or partial aspects of NDEs, as happens with all alternative explanations so far. Such theories should also be able to explain the 65 percent of people who come close to death but do not have an NDE.

Thus far these attempts and others have been unsuccessful in explaining the NDE. Researchers have just not been able to explain away this spiritual phenomenon. It surely seems that the NDE is real.

Summary

The NDE is a widespread phenomenon, with over 22 million adults in the United States having had an NDE. Approximately one person in every eleven in the United States has had an NDE.

The evidence for the reality of the NDE is thousands of interviewees reporting corresponding NDEs to near-death researchers, historical NDEs, Sabom's experiment, childhood NDEs, NDE aftereffects on NDErs, NDE flashforwards, and the lack of verifiable alternative explanations for the NDE.

CHAPTER 3

Pre-Earth Life
and Its Purposes

How often have you heard somebody say life is so short? From the broader perspective of the near-death experience, this is not necessarily an accurate statement. According to information collected from NDEs, we have been around longer than just an earthly lifetime.

Visions and Remembrance of a Pre-Mortal World

Evidence from NDEs concerning a pre-mortal existence is now emerging in near-death studies, with Craig Lundahl publishing the initial work on this topic in 1992. During their NDEs, Betty Eadie, Herman Stulz, Elane Durham, DeLynn, Ranelle Wallace, Angie Fenimore, and Theresa either saw the pre-mortal world or remembered it. Many other NDE accounts suggest the idea of a pre-mortal world when the

NDErs are told their time is not up because the mission they agreed to accomplish while on earth had not been completed.

During her visit to the otherworld in 1973, Eadie found that things came back to her from long before her life on earth, things that had been blocked from her at birth. The fact of a pre-earth life crystallized in her mind. She said, "I was actually relieved to find that the earth is not our natural home, that we did not originate here," as she saw the pre-mortal world during her NDE. In addition, she knew that she had been there before and that each person on earth had been there, too.

Stulz had an NDE in 1896 during which he was told to "go back and finish the work he promised he would do before his spirit left here." It was then that his memory of his pre-mortal life came back to him and he remembered that he had promised to do specific things after he was born.

After a stroke precipitated by a brain tumor in 1976, a superior being taught Durham while she was in the otherworld and let her see herself in the pre-mortal world. She said:

> While he was teaching me about the importance of children he asked me if I would like to see myself before I was born—before I came to earth. I told him I would, and it was as if I were looking in a bathroom mirror that was fogged over. I could see myself, but I couldn't distinguish how my hair was done or my facial characteristics. Seated in what seemed to be a waiting area, I observed that there were five beings around me. Two of them were in a teaching capacity and were strong spiritual beings, and three of them were lesser spiritual beings. They

were guardian angels, or whatever, and the three lesser ones were there to learn—sort of angels in training.

In this pre-mortal environment I saw that I was making all the decisions for my life, the things that I chose to go through. These were things that I wanted to accomplish in order to learn various lessons. There were different choices available to me. I knew, for example, that I was going to be the oldest of the children in my family. There was a choice between three fathers and two mothers; I would have learned equal lessons from all of them. I knew that I would have a physical crisis and would be miraculously healed; and I would have a second health crisis which I would survive.

My life on earth could be prolonged, I understood, by living so as to be in a helping capacity—helping others.

DeLynn, who died after an emergency operation for sinusitis in 1988, discovered it was his choice in the pre-mortal world to suffer the afflictions associated with cystic fibrosis when he came to earth. During his experience he was transported to his pre-mortal existence.

There was a room that I was viewing from above and to the side, but at the same time I was sitting in it. In a sense I was both an observer and a participant. About thirty people were in the room, both men and women, and we were all dressed in the white jump-suit type of garment.

31

An instructor was in the front of the room, and he was teaching about accountability and responsibility—and about pain. He was instructing us about things we had to know in order to come to earth and get our bodies. Then he said, and I'll never forget this: "You can learn lessons one of two ways. You can move through life slowly, and have certain experiences, or there are ways that you can learn the lessons very quickly through pain and disease." He wrote on the board the words: "Cystic Fibrosis," and he turned and asked for volunteers. I was a volunteer; I saw me raise my hand and offer to take the challenge.

The instructor looked at me and agreed to accept me. That was the end of the scene, and it changed forever my perspective of the disease that I previously felt was a plague on my life. No longer did I consider myself a victim. Rather, I was a privileged participant, by choice, in an eternal plan. That plan, if I measure up to the potential of my choice, would allow me to advance in mortal life in the fastest way possible. True, I would not be able to control the inevitable slow deterioration of my mortal body, but I could control how I chose to handle my illness emotionally and psychologically. The specific choice of cystic fibrosis was to help me learn dignity in suffering. My understanding in the eternal sense was complete—I know that I was a powerful, spiritual being that chose to have a short but marvelous, mortal existence.

Wallace saw and experienced the history of our existence before earth during her NDE. She also saw many friends (which she called younger spirits) who had not yet been born and some who had already lived on the earth and died.

During her NDE, Fenimore saw before her birth, a spirit life that seemed to go back to the beginning of the universe. She saw that she was never forced to come to earth and that she knew beforehand what she would face on earth. She even helped to coauthor the course of her life. She was also told her oldest son agreed before he was born to perform specific tasks during his life on earth.

Theresa suffered a heart attack in 1989. During her NDE she went to the otherworld—a world she felt was her real home, where she lived before she came to earth. She said that most of the people she saw she recognized from before she was born. She also saw herself in a pre-mortal state, where she was serving and attending to other people. She chose her whole life, including her family and the difficulties she would have during her lifetime in her pre-earth life. She had wanted to experience everything possible. She said she was aware that these choices would allow her to progress to a higher level.

The implications from some NDE research are that we lived as full-grown spirits in another sphere before arriving on earth. This is suggested particularly by Henry Zollinger, who was crushed by a hay derrick in August 1920, when he stated:

> My Guide then took me and showed me the spirits of the children that would yet come to my family if we would be faithful. They were full grown but not in the same sphere as those which had lived upon the earth.

Children's Visions of Deceased Relatives

It is not unusual to hear of instances where children recognize deceased relatives. Carol tells of such an instance with her young son, Jason.

> For Christmas, I was assembling Books of Remembrance for each of my eleven children. Each book was to contain a picture history of the child from birth to his present age along with pictures of his parents, grandparents, etc. I had pictures scattered all over our large kitchen table.
>
> Jason climbed right up in the middle of them when I tried to lift him down. "Gama!" he said, pointing to a picture of a young woman. "Gama!" he said again. I took him in my arms and showed him the picture again.
>
> "Do you mean Grandma Hazel?" I asked.
>
> "No!" he insisted. "Gama!"
>
> My mother is living and he calls her "Gama Hazo."
>
> The young woman in the picture was his paternal grandmother, Vivian, who had died four years before Jason was born. His living grandmother was much older than the grandmother I thought he had never seen, and the picture was taken at a much younger age. There was no mistake—they did not look alike. This incident indicated to us that his veil of forgetfulness was not complete from a former, heavenly existence.

Norma tells of a similar experience with her young son, Jonathan.

> Then one day when Jonathan and I were in the car—he was about a-year-and-a-half old—he said: "I miss my Father." I told him that his Daddy would be home before we got home. He said: "No, my Father in Heaven. I used to sit and talk with Jesus." It frightened me. I didn't know what to do with this child. I hadn't taught him such things.
>
> When he was about two, he said: "I talked to my grandfather and my uncle, and they told me I had to wait a very long time to come and be with you." I talked to my husband, Kerry, and told him what Jonathan had said. Kerry asked if Jonathan had said what they looked like. We brought Jonathan in to tell us. I had never seen pictures of my husband's dead relatives, nor had I talked about them to Jonathan.
>
> Jonathan described my husband's father and uncle who had died when Kerry was four years old.

In a final experience demonstrating a child's vision of a deceased relative with implications for a pre-mortal world, Johnny tells his mother, Lois, how his great-great-grandfather brought him to earth.

> I was putting three-year-old Johnny to bed when he asked for a bedtime story. For the past few weeks I had been telling him of the adventures of his great-great-grandfather: a colonizer, a soldier, a

community leader. As I started another story, Johnny stopped me and said, "No, tell me of Grandpa Robert." I was surprised. This was my grandpa. I had not told stories of him, and I could not imagine where he had heard his name. He had died before I had even married.

"How do you know about Grandpa Robert?" I asked.

"Well, mamma," he said with reverence, "he's the one who brought me to earth."

Visions of Unborn Children

NDErs have also seen "unborn children" in their NDEs. For example, Calvin saw a group of young children playing together during his journey to the otherworld, and his "eyes fastened upon one and a message was instantly impressed upon his mind that this was his little unborn son."

Katie, a child NDEr in Melvin Morse's study, made new friends in the otherworld, and among them were two young boys, Andy and Mark, who were waiting to be born.

Near-death researchers Bruce Greyson and Nancy Evans Bush reported a case where a woman had an NDE as a result of a car accident. During her NDE a little girl looked up at her and begged her to return to earth. Several years later she had a baby, which she recognized as the little girl.

Mike saw three smaller figures during an NDE that were to be his future children on earth.

Wallace saw a young man named Nathaniel who pleaded

with her to return to her body. Without her as his mother he would not be able to accomplish his mission on earth.

One lady NDEr was shown another child she would have if she returned to life.

Kenneth Ring reported a case in which a person had an NDE during an emergency surgery for a burst appendix. This NDEr reported he had some strange memories after his operation, one of which became clear some twenty-five years later. He suddenly realized that his two children were the children from his 1941 "memory."

As a teenager, the near-death researcher Michelle Sorenson developed a serious infection of the blood and bone as a result of an injury to her leg while skiing, and she nearly died. While out of her body she saw a tall man walking with two children. "The little girl jumped up and down and her curls shook. The other was a boy. I recognized this as being my future family." Years later, walking behind her husband, she saw this exact scene.

While in the otherworld, Kathleen Martinez saw her future child. She said:

> I turned to my right, and I saw this spirit that was going to be my child. The spirit, a male, appeared to be a very old person; in chronological terms he looked to be about ninety, with piercing eyes. He seemed to be very knowledgeable, very intelligent. He said nothing, he looked at me, and we both turned—and I saw this shaft of light. I went down the shaft of light, almost instantaneously, and my spirit seemed to enter my body through the forehead.

In another case, JoAnn stopped breathing during a delicate surgery.

> Instantly, I found myself suspended in the air above my body. I could look down and see everything the doctors and nurses were doing. I saw the heart monitor flat and the nurses stirring about. My doctor moved away from me to allow another doctor to come in. I couldn't understand why everyone appeared to be so worried.

She then found herself transported to an incredible place, where she was surrounded by a brilliant white light. She continued,

> As my senses became alert, I heard a beautiful sound—it was the sound of peace. I cannot describe it with mortal words, only that a powerful feeling of peace permeated my very being. I could hear spiritual beings moving around behind me in a very calm and orderly manner. I don't know where it came from, but all of a sudden I was holding an infant. There was a personage behind me, and he said to me, "This is your daughter, Virginia."
>
> I looked at her and I was so thrilled. Ever since I was a child I had always wanted a blond-haired, blue-eyed little girl. These were the features of the beautiful baby girl I was holding. My fiancé Wade had blond hair and blue eyes.
>
> I looked at her and asked, "Her name is Virginia?"
> The personage behind me said, "Yes."

Virginia was very slow in coming to earth, but she was born healthy, strong and beautiful—mirror-image of the blond-haired, blue-eyed infant I had held when my spirit had left my body during the surgery.

Janet Christensen, the granddaughter of a Canadian woman, told how her grandmother Bertha saw two unborn children in the otherworld who later became her children on earth:

As they moved, the family continued to grow, until 1913 while living in Alberta, Canada, Bertha had given birth to 13 children. After much deliberation, she decided that life was just too difficult for her to bring any more children into the world.

It wasn't long afterwards that Bertha became seriously ill. I don't remember the nature of the illness, only that it was sufficiently serious that a nurse whom Bertha called Sister Edwards came to the home to care for her. In those days, in remote rural communities, going to hospitals was usually out of the question.

With Sister Edwards sitting beside her bed, Bertha suddenly realized she was rising in the air above her bed, the pain and discomfort of a few moments earlier was suddenly gone. As she looked down at her bed, she could see Sister Edwards sitting beside the bed.

Thinking Bertha had died, Sister Edwards later said she wanted to call to the others in the house, but was prompted to do nothing. She had a peaceful feeling that everything would be all right if she just waited a few minutes.

Bertha felt relieved. The pain was gone. She was so full of peace, that she had no particular desire to return to her body.

She was greeted by a woman who escorted her into a large room where she was greeted by many of her departed friends. One was a young man she had befriended and encouraged to develop his artistic talents. He was sitting in front of an easel, painting. Though he was very happy to see Bertha, he quickly returned to his work as though his time was very precious.

Bertha was taken into another room where there were many children. On the far side of the room she saw two little girls, whom she did not know. They were so beautiful she could not look away from them.

"Do you want them?" the guide asked.

"Yes. Oh, yes," she responded quickly. "Can I return to earth life and have them?"

"Yes," said the escort. "That is the purpose of this visit, to let you see them. Now we must return." Bertha returned to her body, much to the relief of Sister Edwards. After recovering from the illness, Bertha told Jonathan [her husband] she wanted more children.

A year later, after moving to Oakley, Idaho, Bertha gave birth to a new little girl whom she named Alberta. Two years later she delivered another little girl, LaVirle. For the remainder of her life, Bertha insisted these were the two little girls she had seen in the large room.

In another NDE account, Jean Scott was pregnant with her third child and was hemorrhaging when she underwent surgery. She related the following:

I felt my spirit kind of gathering to the middle of my body, then draining out the back. I found myself in the corner of the room, floating in mid-air, watching the doctor and nurses trying to revive the body on the operating table.

I felt like I could go back to my body but didn't want to. Suddenly I was aware of a dark tunnel, like a doorway leaving the operating room. I could see it, but the doctors and nurses couldn't. Though I was afraid, I entered the tunnel and found myself traveling very fast towards the far end. I wasn't walking or running, just floating along, very fast. There was a light at the end of the tunnel. It wasn't a blue light, but a warm golden light, very bright. As I neared the end of the tunnel it became very narrow, but I made it through, finding myself in an open place with other people. . . .

Against the doctor's advice, I became pregnant four more times, losing two of the babies prematurely, coming near death again with another of the pregnancies. I knew that several of the people I had seen at the end of the tunnel were to be my future

41

children, so I continued getting pregnant until I felt
I had brought them into the world.

This information definitely suggests people live in another
realm before coming to earth and that relationships on earth
started way before birth.

Purposes and Activities in the Pre-Earth Life

It seems the main purposes of the pre-earth life are for personal development and preparation for the earth life. We were
all individual and mature spirits with an intelligence that was
developed before we even came to earth. Evidently, to develop
and progress we must come to earth and be born.

Among our pre-earth life activities were volunteering to
come to the earth, making covenants with other spirits to
come to earth as family or friends, selecting our missions and
positions for life on the earth, and preparing for the tests and
experiences of life on earth.

Volunteering to Come to Earth. Eadie was taken to a place
in the otherworld where many spirits were preparing for life
on earth. She

> saw how desirous the spirits were of coming to
> earth. They looked upon life here as a school where
> they could learn many things and develop the at-
> tributes they lacked. I was told that we had all de-
> sired to come here, that we had actually chosen

many of our weaknesses and difficult situations in our lives so that we could grow.

Our choice of difficult situations in life is also attested to by Durham, DeLynn, Fenimore, and Theresa, who believed they were unfortunate victims until they realized that they had chosen their difficulties in life to help themselves grow.

Earth Family Covenants. Before coming to earth, we made covenants with others to come to earth as families or friends.

Durham said she had a choice among three fathers and two mothers when she chose her parents. Theresa also said she chose her family.

Eadie was told

> that we had bonded together in the spirit world with certain spirit brothers and sisters—those we felt especially close to. My escorts explained that we covenanted with these spirits to come to earth as family or friends. This spiritual bonding was a result of the love we developed for each other over an eternity of being together. We also chose to come to earth with certain others because of the work we would do together. Some of us wanted to unite in a cause to change certain things on earth, and we could best do it with certain circumstances brought about by selected parents or others. Some of us simply wanted to strengthen a course already set and to pave the way for those who follow. We understood the influences we would have upon

each other in this life and the physical and behavioral attributes we would receive from our families.

Eadie also noted that we bonded with others like family members and friends to help us complete our missions on earth. We needed their help to complete our own missions.

Selecting Missions and Positions for Earth Life. Each of us had the opportunity and agency to select our missions on earth. This was certainly evident to Elane, who made all the decisions for her life while she was in the pre-mortal world. When DeLynn discovered that he had volunteered to have cystic fibrosis while on earth, it changed his whole life. Theresa wanted to experience everything possible while on the earth.

Eadie saw that in the pre-mortal world, we knew about and even chose our missions in life and that our positions in life were based upon the objectives of our missions. She saw that all people volunteered for their positions and stations in the world and receive more help than they know. She says that we came here in stations that are best suited for our spiritual needs. Eadie learned that the choices we made before we came to earth "guide many of our decisions and even many of the seemingly random experiences we have."

Other NDErs, such as Susan Burt, understood that they chose their lives before mortality.

Preparing for Life on Earth. Eadie saw spirits who had not yet come to earth making preparations to go to earth and other spirits leaving to begin their turn on earth.

Eadie also saw many spirits who would come to the earth for a short time, living only hours, or days after their birth. They were as excited as the others, knowing that they had a purpose to fulfill. I understood that their deaths had been appointed before their births—as were all of ours.

Pre-Earth Life Associations

According to many individuals who have the opportunity to view life in the pre-earth life, we had associations with many different individuals.

Wallace saw many friends during her NDE, some who had lived on the earth and died and some who had not yet been born.

Theresa also saw many people during her NDE whom she had associated with in a pre-mortal life, and she learned she had worked with and helped many other people in her pre-mortal life.

During her NDE Eadie recognized three male guides and two close friends as persons and friends she had known before she came to earth. She was told by her guides that they had been with her for eternities in the past. When she met Jesus Christ, she states, "I know that I had known him from the beginning, from long before my earth life, because my spirit remembered him." In a garden reception for Eadie in the otherworld, she met a group of spiritual beings, and she remembered them all from before her earth life.

Christine Monsen spent time with her deceased husband during her NDE, and he told her that when he died he came through the darkness to the light, where Jesus Christ was waiting for him. Christine's husband told her that Jesus Christ had known him since the time before the earth was formed.

Summary

The implication of NDE research is that we lived as full-grown spirits in another realm before our earth life. Apparently the main purposes of pre-earth life are for personal development and preparation for earth life. Among our pre-earth life activities were volunteering to come to earth, making covenants with spirits to come to earth as family and friends, selecting our missions and positions for life on the earth, and preparing for the test and experiences of life on earth. In the pre-earth life, we associated with many people for eternities.

CHAPTER 4

Earth Life
and Its Purposes

The next phase of life is the earth life. It is at this point that each person enters a physical body and takes his or her turn upon the earth, arriving at stations that, from accounts similar to those reported in the previous chapter, best suit their spiritual needs.

Entry into Earth Life

One might ask how a person comes to this earth from the pre-mortal world. One NDE account in particular helps to explain this process:

> When I am pregnant, I have a hormone imbalance that affects my entire glandular system. Although I have sought the best medical advice

available, when I am expecting I become seriously ill, and have lost nine out of my eleven pregnancies.

During one of these pregnancies, I became so weak and tired that I could not walk across the room to call on the phone for help. I was having very heavy contractions and knew that I was not going to make it through that pregnancy. . . .

Only a few moments later, my husband came in to check on me. I was unspeakably relieved that he had come home, and as I tried to ask him for help, I started to miscarry. The physical labor was too much for my body because of my weakened condition. My body stayed right there, but my spirit started leaving. My husband began slapping my face, yet I couldn't respond. I knew that I was passing on, and I watched myself leaving.

Suddenly I started going through dimensions. There is no way to describe what happened. I was moving through our physical dimension into another one. . . .

Before I reached the light, I recalled my life in a sudden flash. It was the most totally exciting, fantastic thing I have ever seen. I saw the time I was brought from heaven to the earth by angels to a body, how I was received at the hospital, and how my parents loved me. From that day until the present, I saw everything that ever happened to me in my life. It was all in an instant, at fantastic speeds and rates, and it was not like a day-to-day procedure. What I saw was like a concept to learn or a trial, experience by experience. My life was arranged

systematically so that everything related to one subject or trial was grouped together. At the end of
each experience I was judged. There was no voice of
judgment, but I knew instantly how the Lord felt
about each thing I had done in my life. I was also
able to perceive how my actions affected everyone
around me. I had never even thought about my influence on others as part of my judgment before,
only what I had done.

In this NDE case, this NDEr saw her arrival in this world.
She was brought to a body by angels much like angels escort
people who die to the post-earth world.

Three-year-old Johnny who was mentioned in the last
chapter said his great-great-grandfather brought him to earth.

It is also at this time that we lose most if not all of our
memory of any world other than the mortal world.

The Operation of Laws on Earth

The earth operates under a body of laws that govern humanity. Ranelle Wallace realized this during her NDE. She discovered that it is only by understanding and living in
accordance with these laws that we are able to receive knowledge and progress in our development. Betty Eadie learned we
can use these laws for our own good or we can suffer the consequences of breaking them. This substantiates what Melvin
Morse stated previously about us inflicting many of society's
problems upon ourselves because we lack understanding
about life and its purpose.

Personal Agency and Development

Betty Eadie learned during her NDE that we are given our personal free agency to act for ourselves while upon the earth, and it is our own actions that will determine the course of our lives. It is also through our actions that we create many of our own rewards or punishments. Of course, we can alter or redirect our lives at any time.

Raymond Moody finds that NDErs are very sensitive to the immediate and long-term consequences of their actions. He says NDErs tell him the life review is similar to seeing your life on a movie screen. NDErs feel their own emotions as well as the emotions of any others who are on this screen with them. They also see how unrelated events become connected and see the full implications of their actions, be they "right" or "wrong." They say that their NDE makes it clear that they will be responsible for all their actions at the end of life.

Moody says he has yet to meet a person who has been through an NDE who doesn't acknowledge that it has made him or her more careful in choosing his or her actions.

Eadie learned that people come to earth for the purpose of furthering their spiritual growth. We are on earth to learn, to experiment, and to make mistakes.

It is through various experiences that we grow and develop. In the pre-earth life we chose a plan to follow while upon the earth that guides many of our decisions and many of the seemingly random experiences in our lives. Everything that happens to us is for a purpose.

The NDEr cited at the beginning of this chapter, who saw herself brought to her body, realized during her NDE that every trial we experience prepares us for the next one and brings us knowledge or wisdom. She recognized how carefully our own individual tests are planned.

Eadie also learned:

> All experience is for our good, and sometimes it takes what we would consider negative experience to help develop our spirits. We were very willing, even anxious, as spirits to accept all of our ailments, illnesses, and accidents here to help better ourselves spiritually.

She adds, "Our most severe challenges will one day reveal themselves to be our greatest teachers."

Angie Fenimore was told that life is supposed to be hard and that all people go through hard parts.

One person told the near-death researcher Melvin Morse that her NDE taught her that "grief is growth." Another person told Morse that everything in the world is interconnected and there is a reason for whatever problem a person faces.

Thelma Huffman, who was seriously injured in an automobile accident, said she was impressed to know that there were important lessons for her to learn during the healing process. She said she later discovered that soul cleansing can come through illness.

What is the best way to develop while on earth? One question that is put to many NDErs during the "life review" seems to give an answer to this question. The question to NDErs is usually phrased "What have you done to benefit or advance the human race?" or "What have you done with your life?" Eadie learned that whatever we become here in mortality is meaningless unless it is done for the benefit of others. Our gifts and talents are given to us to help serve. And in serving others, we develop and grow spiritually.

Thoughts

Eadie's NDE taught her that "there is power in our thoughts. We create our own surroundings by the thoughts we think. . . . If we understood the power of our thoughts, we would guard them more closely." She emphasized again and again in her account that "our thoughts have tremendous power."

Why does Eadie put such an emphasis on thoughts? Because, as Eadie says, "thoughts are deeds." In other words, thoughts lead to actions and, therefore, are very important for all that we do. We tend to become the sum of our thoughts, feelings, and actions; at least, that is what the life review in the NDE suggests. For example, Jayne was told by a being in the otherworld that what really matters is how a person thinks. Our thoughts and actions end up shaping the character of our spirit that will go to the post-mortal world at death.

The effects of our thoughts on our behavior and the course of our lives were demonstrated by some comments made by Barbara to the near-death researcher Kenneth Ring, when she reflected on what her NDE had taught her. She said she had spent 31 years acting good because she thought she was very bad, and that if people found out what she really was like, they would reject her. She felt that if people thought she was a good person they would like and accept her. So she tried to be good to fool them. It was not until after she returned from her NDE that she realized she was a good person, and did not have to put on an act.

Purposes of Earth Life

An examination of the findings from near-death research and various NDE cases suggest the meaning and purposes of life. NDEs tell us the major purposes of life are to love and serve others, to gain knowledge, to grow spiritually, and to fulfill one's life mission. Often mentioned in connection with one's life mission is family. Let us examine each of these purposes more closely.

Love and Serve Others. Universally, NDErs found that God loves each of us unequivocally—no matter who we are, how we live, or what our religion. Almost every NDEr stresses the importance in this life of trying to cultivate love for others. Ranelle Wallace learned that "love is the power of life." She also learned during her NDE that loving and helping people is the key. Her deceased grandmother told her to "tell everybody that the key is love."

Ernest Martinez's spiritual guide in the other world told him that

> without love nothing in all the universe could stand. Without love, everything would fall into decay and dissolution. . . .
>
> Not until a human has learned to love all others without hating anyone is he or she able to progress toward the Light. In this higher sphere, my son, love

is light, and light is love. Those who do not love must move in dark places where they are apt to lose their way completely.

Carol was told by Jesus during her NDE that "Divine Love is the one great power that moves the universe. Divine Love is the force that makes men and women think and do those things that create peace and goodwill."

Elizabeth Marie felt the love of Jesus physically as he embraced her. It was extremely intense and traveled from her toes to her head, filling her entire body. She said that no words could adequately describe this great love—it was beyond belief.

Debbie also felt total love from Christ. She said, "He loved me—it was a love that I had not felt previously nor since, anyplace on earth."

Moody points out that after the NDE, almost all NDErs "say that love is the most important thing in life." Many of the NDErs "say it is why we are here. Most find it the hallmark of happiness and fulfillment, with other values paling beside it." Moody also says many people sense, when asked what is going on in their hearts by the "being" during the life review of the NDE, that the simple acts of kindness that come from the heart are the ones that are most important because they are most sincere.

One NDEr said:

Before the accident I was a very competitive person, always wanting the highest grade, the best job, the most money. I think I'm different now. I think

I love and appreciate other people more and have a stronger desire to do things for others.

According to Huffman:

I learned that the most important thing we can do on this earth is to show consideration, love and kindness to others. There are no bonuses for position alone, nor power and wealth. We are judged by how we treat people, and what we do for others.

Eadie put it this way:

Above all, I was shown that love is supreme. I saw that truly without love we are nothing. We are here to help each other, to care for each other, to understand, forgive, and serve one another. We are here to have love for every person born on earth.

She further wrote that people on the earth are all collectively bonded to each other, united in one supreme purpose of learning to love one another. This includes seeing the poor just as worthy of our esteem as the rich and accepting all others, even those who may be different from us. Eventually we will have to account for how we have treated others.

Eadie also wrote:

The only thing we can take with us from this life is the good that we have done to others. I saw that all of our good deeds and kind words will come back to bless us a hundred-fold after this life. Our strength will be found in our charity.

John Stirling said:

It's the way I feel about people, now, and life in general—that we are all part of the same plan. We are all part of the same program; the greatest value for any of us is to try and help another person in their situation. We shouldn't interfere with others negatively, nor should we hurt another person. We should not, in any way, detract from a life. Rather we should add to other people's lives. . . . We get carried away with the temporal aspects of our own situations. We become involved in seeking money, or newer cars, or nicer clothes, or something, and we forget the things that, I believe, the Savior was trying to teach—concerning love and his way of love, his way of understanding. We should not judge our fellow beings, but we should love them, and serve them.

One woman said our relationships with other people and the caring and compassion and love we have for them is most important. She added that love is the answer to everything.

Elane Durham, during her NDE, was informed:

56

My life on earth could be prolonged, I understood, by living so as to be in a helping capacity—helping others. That might not sound like a big deal here and now, but over there it was just understood that helping others is a primary purpose.

During his NDE, Harold was asked what he had done to benefit or advance the human race. He discovered that what he had counted in life as important was nothing. Bill discovered it was the little things in life (as defined by most people) that are really important, "a hurt child that you helped or just to stop to say hello to a shut-in." Spencer learned, "It's the purpose of my life to pass on as much positiveness as I can every day of my life with any person I meet."

DeLynn was told that if he chose to return to his body, "you have the obligation to teach those principles (accountability and responsibility) to your family and your employees."

Dallas's experience "helped me to understand that the important accomplishments in this life are not related to material things. They are related to how we help others, to how we interact with family and friends, and to the love we extend to others."

Elizabeth Marie was told she had to return to help others who had lost their way. She reported that

He held me in His arms . . . and the love I felt was beyond belief. And while I was embraced by Him and felt of His love, He asked me if I would help others to come back to Him. I said I would.

> Since my experience, I haven't known who it was
> I was supposed to help. I've wondered if it was one
> person, or many persons. I understood that it was
> to help someone, or several people, who had lost
> their way, to return to His presence. . . .

Many individuals who returned to their bodies following their NDEs knew they had a mission to fill, that this mission entailed a work that they needed to complete, but they often did not know what that mission was, only that the work had something to do with helping others in some way.

Yellow Face, a chief in a Cree tribe from northeastern Saskatchewan, was given a very specific charge. He reported having an NDE in 1909 in which he was told to find a book containing the history of his people. He was visited by a man who told him to wrap his blanket around him and to go with him on a journey.

> I went right off, and looked down on my body
> when I went with this visitor—saw an Indian there
> wrapped in his blankets, and I wondered how it was
> that I was living and yet it was I there wrapped in
> my own blankets. I wondered if anyone would
> come along and bury my body before I returned.

He reported that members of his village watched over his body, checking it for any signs of life.

> He was watched for five days and only above his
> heart was there a small warm place. On the end of
> the fifth day he came to, and he called all his coun-

58

cil together and told them he had been into a country where he saw his forefathers, walked with them, talked with them; and they told him he would not yet die, for he would come back to the earth and that he was to send all over the country until he found a people who had a book in which was recorded the history of the many people he had been with in the spirit world. . . .

Before coming to the earth, many individuals apparently made commitments to do things that can be done only on earth. Possibly the pressures of earth life resulted in these commitments being forgotten or displaced by other concerns. In any event, it was not until they returned to the world of spirits during their NDE that their commitments were "remembered." There many individuals met deceased relatives who not only reminded them of their obligations to them, but encouraged them to fulfill them. In some cases they were pleaded with to return to earth to do specific things.

Morse has also listed messages given exclusively to children NDErs, and these certainly emphasize loving and serving others:

- Love your neighbor and cherish life.
- Do unto others as you would have them do unto you.
- Clean up your own mess.
- Be the best that you can be.
- Contribute to society.
- Be nice, kind, and loving.

Gain Knowledge. Eadie noted that the earth is a temporary abode for our schooling and observed that the many spirits preparing for life on earth looked upon this life as a school where they would learn many things and develop attributes they lacked.

During Ingrid's NDE, her guardian angel told her that everything that happened to her was part of the testing program of earth and that in a very real sense, earth is a schoolhouse where people have to pass certain tests before they can advance to the next grade.

We mentioned previously that Ring had stated that the basic message NDErs come away with is that "knowledge" and love are what are really important.

Moody also noted in his first book that many NDErs he spoke with emphasized the importance of seeking knowledge. He wrote, "During their experiences, it was intimated to them that the acquisition of knowledge continues even in the afterlife." In 1988 Moody wrote that NDErs realize after reviewing their lives that a person's knowledge goes with him or her at the time of death, and learning continues after a person dies. Some of them even describe a realm of the afterlife that is designated specifically for the pursuit of knowledge.

Eadie was told that it is important to acquire knowledge while in the flesh and that the more knowledge a person acquires here, the further and faster he or she will progress in the next world. She was also told that because of a lack of knowledge or belief, some spirits are virtual prisoners of this earth. For example, those who die as atheists or those who are bonded to the world because of greed, bodily appetites, or other earthly commitments find it difficult to move on, and they become earthbound.

Spiritual Growth. Eadie learned people come to earth for the purpose of furthering their spiritual growth. On the earth, everything is done for the growth of the spirit. People are on the earth to learn, to experiment, and to make mistakes. It is through serving others that we grow spiritually.

Other NDErs have stressed the importance of spiritual growth, and in one case, Fay Alvey was told by her deceased father to change her ways and live her religion, and that she had to be more righteous. One NDEr said the experience showed that spirituality is important; another NDEr now tries to do things that have more meaning, that make the mind and soul feel better; and a third NDEr, an elderly woman, said we are "given the opportunity to learn and grow spiritually and get prepared for the next life." Most NDErs have a heightened sense of spiritual purpose after their NDEs.

Michael B. Sabom found that the religious views of persons who experienced an NDE were strengthened by their NDEs, and this was evidenced by a marked increase in formal religious activity or personal commitment. George Gallup Jr. also said one of the main results of NDEs was a strengthening of personal religious beliefs. Ring concluded in his study that the NDE is a spiritual experience that can produce spiritual behavior. Ring differentiates between religious and spiritual with a saying by a wise man: "A religious person follows the teachings of his church, whereas the spiritual person follows the guidance of his soul."

Moody probably best described the message for spiritual or religious growth when he wrote that both the believers and nonbelievers say after their NDEs that they do believe in God and have a greater spiritual appreciation. Both groups come out of an NDE saying that religion concerns your ability to love and that denominations do not count.

A Life Mission. One of the major findings of NDE research is that each person's life has a purpose.

Many individuals who have had in-depth NDEs returned from the otherworld with a strong sense of mission. While most were not aware of exactly what they were supposed to accomplish, they did realize that whatever it was, it is an essential part of their earthly lives. For example, when Jacob Hamblin died and tried to join his father in the spirit world, he was told by his father that it was not time. When he asked why, his father answered, "Your work is not yet done." When Isaac Black was told that he had to go back, that his work on earth was not finished, he wept. His guardian angel assured him that he could return once his work was completed. Part of the unfinished work had to do with his family. They were too young and needed him.

Gallup found that after an NDE some NDErs felt that God had a plan for their lives. Morse says, "The feeling that there is a purpose to life is one of the results of many childhood NDEs."

After being told her death was premature and it was not yet her time, Eadie felt her time to die would come when her mission, her purpose, her meaning in this life, was accomplished.

Other NDErs have had similar experiences. For example, Karl Muecke said a voice told him that he was to return to life since he had a special mission to perform. Jennette was told that she must go back because her work was not yet done. Cindi, a young NDEr, was told by her deceased grandfather to go back to her body because she had more work to do. While in the otherworld Ronna Lackey understood that she had chosen to live at this time and had promised to do certain work, and because of that realization she returned to life. Sharon McQueen, when given a choice to stay in the otherworld or return, said she understood there was a mission for her to fill or something special to do if she returned, so she chose to return.

Perhaps the point to be made here is best summed up with the words of Neddie Pitcher. She was told by a personage in the otherworld, whom she believed was her Father in Heaven, that she would know her mission in life as time went on. This statement implies that all people have a purpose or some mission in this earthly life.

Often family is part of a person's mission on earth. This is demonstrated by the number of times NDErs have returned to their bodies because they felt they had responsibilities to help their families. Here is a description of an NDE illustrating this point, as told by a daughter:

> My mother Margaret, was a young lady when her appendix ruptured. Later, peritonitis set in and she died.
>
> When she left her body, she was met by a heavenly being who told her that she had a decision to make. Because her mother [Margaret's mother] had previously passed away, leaving a large family, her father needed her very much. She was also aware that her older sister and brothers were bearing great responsibilities and needed her help.

The person who met her said, "You can go back into your body, or remain here. It is your choice."

My mother looked around her and saw that everything was beautiful and peaceful. She was overwhelmed with the joy and relief that would have been hers if she had stayed there. Mother also saw her father weeping and trying to comfort her grieving brothers and sisters.

After serious consideration, she felt her family needed her in mortality. . . .

Morse pointed out that family was the purpose for a return to life in the case of Rick, a child NDEr. He said Rick felt he lived because he was supposed to have a loving relationship with his family.

Another significant aspect of the work an individual must complete has to do with the rearing of children. Some individuals were told that they should return to their families, as they were not needed just then, and besides, their responsibilities as earthly parents had not yet been fulfilled. For example, a young woman was told by messengers:

Satan had such great power on earth that her children needed their mother to build strong faith.

Another woman reported that she was told, "Go back, go back. Your kids and a lot of people are going to need you. We don't need you now!"

Iris Lemoy saw figures of people, dressed in shrouds,

coming toward her and calling her by name. This man with a white beard told me to go back—your family still needs you—enjoy your life. This beautiful man was my grandfather who had died two years before I was born.

A woman, delighted to meet her sister, who had been killed many years earlier, told her sister, "I am so happy to be here!" Her sister answered, " 'I know but you can't stay. You must go back to your five reasons.' With that she named each of my five children. I had no choice.' "

During her NDE, Jean was asked, "Is there anyone to take care of your children if you stay?" She told them that there wasn't anyone else. They then told her that she had to return.

Ashford, during his NDE, was asked by a being of light if he wanted to live. He was tempted to say no, then thought about his family.

I dearly loved my wife. It wouldn't be fair to leave her alone with all the problems and two young girls still to raise. I realized my oldest daughter would need me more now than ever before. My son needed my love and encouragement.

Mary Evans saw her husband awaiting her, but as she attempted to join him, he told her, "No! Not yet! Go back." She realized that it was for the sake of their mentally handicapped daughter.

The family is the basic unit both on earth and in the spirit world. This basic unit is formed of unique spirits who elected to join as families in the pre-mortal world. Part of the process of creating these families involved commitments made by parents to their children, children to their parents, children to each other, and all family members to more distant relatives. During NDEs, these commitments and promises are recounted and the individual "knows" that he or she has further work to do on earth.

Alfred, a young father, was reminded of the eternal nature of his family when his deceased wife visited him as he lay in his bed, close to death.

It [an angelic form] gently floated to my bedside, and looking it in the face, I saw it was my arisen wife! She knelt down by the bedside, exactly where she had been accustomed to kneel, morning and evening, when in the body. Addressing me in the sweetest accents, she said:

"Alfred, you must not think of giving up. You have still a great work to do, and you must endeavor to do it.

"Then there are the children. They need all the help and care you can render them.

"No; you must never give up. Be brave, and work your way through all your trials and difficulties. You will receive such help as will enable you to come off victorious at last. I may not tarry longer. Adieu! Adieu!"

She waved her hand as she floated away and vanished out of sight.

Joyce Brown's life was plagued with serious health problems and adversity. She became so depressed that she no longer desired to live and literally willed herself to die. Then she experienced an extensive NDE during which she learned that life is precious, that it's a gift from God, and that we have no right to end it. She found out that one cannot escape one's problems through suicide, one takes them with you. She discovered that we all have specific missions to accomplish on earth and that our missions are intertwined with the life missions of many other beings. If we die prematurely, our missions are aborted and the missions of others are adversely affected. Our lives could have touched others in significant ways, much like the ripples caused by a pebble tossed into a pond, with those lives touching others, and on and on.

She witnessed the short- and long-range impact of another person's suicide, that of a young woman. This young woman saw and felt the immediate pain and anguish her parents, her brother and sisters, grandparents, friends, and associates at school experienced because of her suicide. She even experienced the pain of total strangers who read about the young woman's death and grieved the death of someone so young. She saw the young woman trying to dissuade others from making the same mistake, being totally distressed when she could not reach them. She saw how the young woman's suicide caused others to consider it as a way out for them. Joyce watched the effects of this single act spread and the numerous lives that were altered because of it. She learned that everyone has a great mission to fulfill, lives to touch, children to bear. The young woman's children were to have had children and their children to have children. Many, many lives would not be the way they were originally planned and designed because of what this one young woman had done. Her act had eternal consequences which could not be reversed. The lessons she could have learned, the blessings she could have earned, the lives she could have touched for good, were forfeited. Those individuals who could have been hers to rear would now have to be reared by others. Their lives would go on, they would complete their missions, but not as originally planned. There was no going back. But through Joyce, others might be dissuaded from making the same tragic mistake.

This young woman's message to us is, life is precious. We all have important missions to perform here on earth and our lives affect many individuals here on earth and those yet to come to earth in ways we cannot imagine. Suicide is never the answer to any problem.

Joyce also learned that adversity has a purpose. The pain and anguish associated with whatever is impacting on us, it is not a punishment. Adversity can help us to grow, to develop those qualities needed to accomplish our mission on earth. Through adversity we can develop compassion, empathy, and tolerance. It is like a refiner's fire, helping us to purify, strengthen, and grow. If we are to accomplish our mission on earth, we need others and they need us. Suicide, while it will not stop the grand purpose of earth life, can certainly disrupt it.

Materialism and Earth Life

It is quite evident from NDE research that materialism is not one of the purposes of earth life. After their NDEs, NDErs become less status conscious and materialistic. Ring's research shows that NDErs are people who enjoy their possessions but are not particularly attached to them and certainly do not live for them. Ring found that in a hierarchy of NDE values, material things did not rank very high.

Lee Nelson noted a theme that recurs in several of his documented NDEs:

> Wealth, power, position in the church, even attendance at church meetings, didn't seem to matter—only what one did to improve conditions and lighten the burdens of others. Christian service and charity were far ahead of anything else in winning approval and peace for those entering the world of spirits.

Kent Johnson said:

> I also received the strong impression that positions at work, in society and in the church are not important at all. What matters is how we treat people, whether or not we are kind to them and what kind of relationship we build with our families.

Katrina said:

> Since that experience I haven't felt suicidal at all. Everything has changed. I'm not interested in money anymore. I wanted money to buy security, to be safe, in a nice house, with an education.

Moody describes a man he calls Mark who was obsessed with money and social position all his life. Then he suffered

a severe heart attack in his mid-forties. After Mark was revived his perspective on life completely changed. All the
things that had driven Mark before his heart attack were now
far below family, friendships, and knowledge on his list of
priorities.

Mr. Dippong said a great desire for spiritual understanding and to see conditions in the world improve replaced his
interest in material wealth and possessions.

Hank reported:

> I realized that there are things that every person
> is sent to earth to realize and to learn. For instance,
> to share more love, to be more loving toward one
> another. To discover that the most important thing
> is human relationships and love and not materialis-
> tic things. And to realize that every single thing that
> you do in your life is recorded and that even though
> you pass it by not thinking at the time, it always
> comes up later.

A guardian angel told Ingrid during her NDE that the reason it was difficult for humans and angels to work together is
that humans "give too much thought to the material things of
earth and too little thought to the everlasting virtues and
truths."

What is particularly disconcerting about materialism is
that it can stop spiritual growth. Betty Eadie saw how dam-
aging the lust for things in the world is. She said, "All real
growth occurs spiritually, and worldly things like possessions
and rampant appetites smother the spirit."

The Future of the Earth

What does the future hold for the earth? We gain some insight into the earth's future by examining NDE prophetic visions.

In chapter 2 we described two types of flashforwards, one identified by Kenneth Ring and the other by Craig Lundahl. A third type of flashforward investigated and labeled by Ring is the "prophetic vision." This type of flashforward is different from the other two types in that it has a world or global focus and pertains to a picture of the earth's future rather than pertaining solely to the personal future of an individual. Ring also reported that prophetic visions were highly consistent from person to person.

A general scenario of the prophetic vision as reproduced by Ring follows:

> There is, first of all, a sense of having total knowledge, but specifically one is aware of seeing the entirety of the earth's evolution and history, from the beginning to the end of time. The future scenario, however, is usually of short duration, seldom extending much beyond the beginning of the twenty-first century. The individual reports that in this decade there will be an increasing incidence of earthquakes, volcanic activity and generally massive geophysical changes. There will be resultant disturbances in weather patterns and food supplies. The world economic system will collapse, and the possibility of nuclear war or accident is very great (respondents are not agreed on whether a nuclear

catastrophe will occur). All of these events are transitional rather than ultimate, however, and they will be followed by a new era in human history, marked by human brotherhood, universal love and world peace. Though many will die, the earth will live.

An illustration of a prophetic vision is given by Reinee Pasarow, who had an NDE in 1967:

The vision of the future I received during my near-death experience was one of tremendous upheaval in the world as a result of our general ignorance of the "true" reality. I was informed that mankind was breaking the laws of the universe and as a result of this would suffer. This suffering was not due to the vengeance of an indignant God but rather like the pain one might suffer as a result of arrogantly defying the law of gravity. It was to be an inevitable educational cleansing of the earth that would creep up upon its inhabitants, who would try to hide blindly in the institutions of law, science, and religion. Mankind, I was told, was being consumed by the cancers of arrogance, materialism, racism, chauvinism, and separatist thinking. I saw sense turning to nonsense, and calamity, in the end, turning to providence.

At the end of this general period of transition, mankind was to be "born again," with a new sense of his place in the universe. The birth process, however, as in all the kingdoms, was exquisitely painful. Mankind would emerge humbled yet educated, peaceful, and, at last, unified.

Another prophetic vision came from a man who had an NDE in 1943. He said we can expect in the future some of nature's most disastrous upheavals. But we will experience more than environmental disasters; we will also experience major disruptions in relationships between individuals, families, and nations. These cataclysms will be unparalleled in human history unless we stop being so materialistic and learn to love ourselves and others.

During Christine Monsen's NDE in 1987, she saw the earth enveloped in layers of dark haze that was growing thicker as she watched. Her deceased husband, who was present, explained that it was evil that darkens the earth and it will continue to spread until the whole earth is covered and that terrible turmoil is ahead.

Thus these NDE prophetic visions show the future of the earth into the beginning of the twenty-first century and suggest an increasing incidence of upheaval and destruction in the world, both of a social and a natural nature. This transitional period will be followed by a new era of human history characterized by love and peace.

Summary

Earth life begins with the assumption of a physical body on the earth. The earth operates under a body of laws, and while here, a person must live within these laws or suffer the consequences of breaking them.

All people on earth have the freedom to act for themselves. Their actions determine the course of their lives. People are on the earth to further their spiritual growth, and it is through their plans for life that they grow and develop. Everything that happens to an individual is for a purpose. Meaningful and significant growth occurs primarily by serving others.

A person's thoughts lead to actions, and it is those thoughts and actions that shape the character of a person.

The purpose of earth life is to love and serve others, to gain knowledge, to grow spiritually, and to fulfill one's life mission. Materialism is not one of the purposes of earth life. On the contrary, it inhibits growth and development.

In the future, according to NDE prophetic visions, the earth will experience an increasing incidence of upheaval and destruction, both of social and natural natures. This transitional period will be followed by a new era of human history characterized by love and peace.

CHAPTER 5

The Death Transition

Is there an afterlife? For most of the core NDErs in Kenneth Ring's study, the idea of life after death becomes not merely highly probable, but a veritable certainty. This perception reflects the findings of a number of NDE researchers on the aftereffects of the NDE.

NDEs essentially tell NDErs that they are not snuffed out of existence by death. As the author Lee Nelson has pointed out, "This is important because—to a large degree—how we view death determines how we live life."

Generally, the feelings of NDErs about an afterlife are expressed in this statement by Elizabeth Whitehead:

> Because of what had just happened I no longer just believed in an afterlife. I knew for a surety there was life beyond death because I had just been there.

Death—The Transition to Another State

"Death is nothing to fear" is easier said than done. Yet probably the most frequently mentioned aftereffect of the NDE on the NDEr is the statement "I lost all fear of death" or "I am not afraid to die anymore." After the experience, Annette Long stated, "My fear of death is gone." In other words, NDErs in almost every case (if not all cases) lose their fear of death after an NDE. It is, as they say, nothing to fear. Betty Eadie was told by her guides in the otherworld that when we die "we experience nothing more than a transition to another state."

From the accounts cited in NDE research there is enough information to describe what happens while a person is dying. These events are (1) pain, (2) a deathbed vision, (3) spirit separation, and (4) peace. More specifically, these events include pain that may precede the death of a person, the deathbed vision that may precede death, the spirit separation that may be a slow separation or be triggered quickly by severe physical trauma, the separation of the person's spirit from the physical body to a space above the body, where the body is seen by the deceased person, the elimination of pain as the spirit leaves the body, and the peace that accompanies the actual experience of dying. The dying process is followed by the movement to the otherworld in the accompaniment of an angel or a being sent to accompany the person following physical death.

Pain. A person who is dying will generally experience some pain at the beginning of the dying process. Many NDErs describe the pain they experience before their NDE. One example is this description:

> Eventually, I drank so much that my bowels began to cringe with excruciating pain. Never in my life had I experienced such agony. My companion and I had been walking and were on the outskirts of our apartment complex, when suddenly the pain became so overwhelming that I doubled over, grasping my stomach and screaming. My companion bent and lifted me to his shoulder, carrying me all the way to our apartment. . . .
>
> By the time we reached our rooms, my screaming had given way to sobbing out the words, "I want to die! I want to die! I want to die!" . . .
>
> I had been gasping because of the pain, but somehow I just gave up and felt my last breath leave my mouth. At that instant, all the pain was gone, and I was flying at an enormous speed through darkness into a light. . . .

George Gallup notes that the fears and anticipation of pain preceding near death are always worse than undergoing death. Respondents to his surveys reported that undergoing death is more pleasant than life itself.

It is also possible that persons dying from a car accident, for instance, may not experience any pain as they die.

Deathbed Visions. Many times before death a person will experience what is called a "deathbed vision." Deathbed visions are accounts of dying people who report seeing deceased relatives and friends and into the world of spirits before dying.

A typical deathbed vision is the following case of a sixty-year-old woman dying of intestinal cancer, cited by the near-death researchers Karlis Osis and Erlendur Haraldsson:

> All of a sudden [the doctor reports] she opened her eyes. She called her [deceased] husband by name and said she was coming to him. She had the most peaceful, nicest smile just as if she were going to the arms of someone she thought a great deal of. She said, "Guy, I am coming." She didn't seem to realize I was there. It was almost as if she were in another world. It was as if something beautiful had opened up to her; she was experiencing something so wonderful and beautiful.

In another deathbed vision case, a woman in the last seconds of life looked up and said, "There's Bill," and then died. Unbeknownst to her, her brother, Bill, had died just the week before.

Triggering Spirit Separation. The separation of the spirit from the body during death can be a slow separation or be triggered quickly by severe physical trauma, as that caused by a serious automobile accident.

The NDEr Betty Eadie was told by her guides that at death the spirit can gradually slip from the body or can leave the body quickly. A slow separation is demonstrated by the first description of spirit separation cited under the subtitle "Spirit Separation." A quick traumatic death is illustrated by

78

the comments of James Niitsuma, who said, "Just before the car rolled, as it turned, my spirit left my body, and I didn't feel anything."

Spirit Separation. Next in the process of dying is the actual separation of the person's spirit from the physical body. One person described this separation:

> Suddenly my body was tingling all over. It felt like someone was pulling on me. My spirit began to come out of my body, starting at the head then working down to my feet. I remember slowly rising above my body, then turning over so I could look down at myself. The pain and sickness were gone. I felt happy. I felt very good.

In another description, Joy Melvin said in an interview:

> As I lay there, my face felt warm, and I felt as though I were moving my head from side to side, like I was saying no, and yet my head didn't feel like it was moving on the couch. The next thing I knew, it felt really weird, I just came out here. . . . At the top of my head, in my head area. It happened so fast. I felt myself come out. . . .

Another NDEr, Stephanie LaRue, said that "All of a sudden, within the blink of an eye, I left my body. It was so fast and so natural. I wasn't afraid—of course I didn't know that this was death." She knew she had left her body because she turned around and saw herself in bed.

Many of these descriptions by NDErs also suggest that after the separation from the body the deceased person is usually in the air above the body, where he or she can see it.

At the time of the separation of the spirit from the body, someone in the presence of the dying person may see an essence or the spirit leave the dying person's body. There are many cases of people seeing this essence leave the body of a dying person.

Melvin Morse cites a case where a mother saw her son's spirit leave his body:

> I was hysterical. Doctors ran into the room and I was ushered out while the doctors worked over his body. I could watch through glass windows in the hall as they did their work. I was crying because I expected the worst.
>
> Suddenly I saw him fly right out of his body! I could see this misty wisp go right up. He moved around near the ceiling for a few seconds and then he just disappeared! One of the doctors came out and told me that they had gotten him back but I knew they hadn't. I told him that I had just seen my boy leave his body and the doctor asked if I would like to sit down. A few moments later another doctor came out and announced that he had died.

No Pain When Leaving Physical Body. There is ample evidence from NDE research of little pain being experienced when a dying person leaves the body. The words of Ella Jensen illustrate this point: "There was practically no pain on leaving the body in death but the intense pain was almost unbearable in coming back to life." In fact, all reported NDE cases indicate that once a person has left the body he or she does not have any pain whatsoever. The cases mentioned under "Spirit Separation" do not suggest that any pain occurs when a dying person leaves the body.

Peace. One of the major experiences at the time of death is the feeling of peace felt by a person. A woman remarked after recovering from a heart attack:

> I began to experience the most wonderful feelings. I couldn't feel a thing in the world except peace, comfort, ease—just quietness. I felt that all my troubles were gone, and I thought to myself, "Well how quiet and peaceful, and I don't hurt at all."

Raymond Moody cites another NDE case where a man recalls:

> I just had a nice, great feeling of solitude and peace. . . . It was beautiful, and I was at such peace in my mind.

Journey to the World of Light. At the end of the process of dying or shortly thereafter, the deceased person moves to the world of light in the accompaniment of a being or an angel sent to accompany the dead. Many NDErs meet angels during an NDE. These angels function as guides, companions, or escorts to people as they travel up the tunnel on their journey to the light or in their entrance into the afterlife. This is suggested by John Peterson, who described his death experience in these words:

> It was between ten and eleven o'clock that a visitor suddenly made his appearance in the room, and standing by the couch on which I lay, placed his hand on my head and asked if I were ready to go? I answered, "Yes," and just at that instant I seemed to stand upon the floor, my body lying on the bed. I looked around to see if my father could see us, but he seemed too interested in reading to have noticed us. We started off on our journey through space, seemingly with the rapidity of lightning (for I can make no other comparison). I asked my guide who he was. He answered that he was one of the guardian angels sent to bring the dead.

After dying, however, a person may choose to remain on the earth until his or her body is buried. Eadie learned that "most spirits choose to remain on earth for a short time and comfort their loved ones." One NDEr, Peter Johnson, states that he was informed in the otherworld that his first duty would be to watch his body until it had been disposed of because this was necessary knowledge for him to have for the resurrection.

Summary

Probably the most frequently mentioned aftereffect of the NDE is that dying is nothing to fear. As Doreen Edwards stated flatly, "The terror I had of death is gone." In almost every case, if not all cases, NDErs lose their fear of death after their NDE. The specific events in the process of dying suggest that dying is a relatively painless, quick, and simple process. As Betty Eadie was told by her guides in the other-world, when a person is dying he or she is experiencing nothing more than a transition to another state.

The process of dying may include pain, a deathbed vision, a slow or quick spirit separation, the person's spirit in the air above the body where the body is viewed by the deceased person, little or no pain as the spirit leaves the body, peace, and a movement to the world of light in the accompaniment of a being or angel sent to bring the dead.

CHAPTER 6

Death: Crossing into
the World of Light

The results from studies conducted by a growing number of near-death researchers suggest those who die encounter an extradimensional realm of reality. George Gallup Jr.'s national survey uncovered evidence that points toward a superparallel universe of some sort.

As deceased individuals enter the otherworld, they may experience something like a veil closing between themselves and others left behind on the earth. They will experience what some have called a "new birth" or "rebirth" in a new location. A pregnant woman said, "Suddenly I started going through dimensions. There is no way to describe what happened. I was moving through our physical dimension into another one."

This new location is beautiful. Mr. Dippong said he found himself in a very beautiful location, vastly more beautiful than anything he had experienced on earth, but at the same time familiar, as though he had always been aware of its existence. He felt there were no words in any language to describe its beauty, and that the greatest literary works by men and women could merely portray a shadow of its glory.

The primary fear of death for most people is a fear of pain and what, if anything, occurs after death. Death has always been thought of as the great unknown. However, thousands of individuals just like Mr. Dippong have lived, died, and returned to report on what they have seen while they were clinically dead. There are also countless individuals who have caught glimpses into the next world just before they died and whose observations and reactions were recorded. The rich detail in these accounts does much to alleviate the fears and uncertainties about death that plague so many people today.

What is it like to die? In studying thousands of recorded cases, the answer is clear. Dying may be very painful, but death is not. In fact, death itself is beautiful. One man in his twenties was dying from gunshot wounds in his abdomen. When he saw Jesus and felt he was going with him, his mood changed from fear to acceptance, from agony to peace, and he was not afraid to die.

Joy Snell, a nurse who worked with dying patients, reported two cases where the vision her patients saw removed all their pain and suffering and left them in peace and serenity as they died.

> I recall the death of a woman who was the victim of that most dreadful disease, malignant cancer. Her sufferings were excruciating, and she prayed earnestly that death might speedily come and end her agony. Suddenly her sufferings appeared to cease; the expression of her face, which a moment before had been distorted by pain,

changed to one of radiant joy. Gazing upwards, with glad light in her eyes, she raised her hands and exclaimed: "Oh, mother dear, you have come to take me home. I am so glad!" And in another moment her physical life ceased.

The memory of another death which occurred about the same time comes back to me. It was that of an old soldier who was in the last stages of tuberculosis, brought on by exposure while fighting his country's battles. He was brave and patient but had frequent paroxysms of pain that were almost unendurable, and he longed for the relief which he knew death alone could bring him. One of these spasms had seized upon him, and his features were convulsed with agony as he fought for breath, when he suddenly grew calm. A smile lit up his face, and, looking upwards, he exclaimed, with a ring of joy in his voice, "Marion, my daughter!" Then he died.

His brother and sister were at the bedside. The sister said to the brother: "He saw Marion, his favorite daughter. She came and took him where he will suffer no more." And she added fervently: "Thank God! He has found rest at last."

One young woman clung desperately to life. She did not want to die and leave her two small children. She was also very fearful of death. As she slipped ever closer to death she became hysterical:

"I don't want to die," she screamed. "I don't want to leave my children. Why can't someone help me? I don't want to die."

Her screams tore the emotions of those who loved her. They tried to comfort her. (Hers was a very close family and everyone except her father who had died several years before were at her side.) But nothing they could say helped. The hysterical sobbing only grew worse. Nurses on the floor heard and summoned the resident physician. He rushed to help in the only way he could—he gave her a hypo to plunge her into unconsciousness.

She was out for seven hours. When the drug wore off, her devoted family was still huddled near, loving her, praying, hoping they could find some way to help.

But the sick woman woke with a smile on her face. "I am sorry I acted so badly," she said. "Everything's all right now. I've seen Dad. He came and told me that there's nothing to be afraid of. He promised that he'd stay with me every minute and hold my hand. Don't worry about me. I'm all right now."

There were no more hysterics. That night the girl slipped over into the next life. There was a smile on her face and one hand was outstretched.

This young dying mother was surrounded by family on both sides. This realization eliminated all her fears of death and left her with a sense of peace. For some individuals, what they see is so beautiful that they no longer desire to live. The following account is about a woman who had just given birth and was suffering from heart failure.

> Suddenly she looked eagerly toward one part of the room, a radiant smile illuminating her whole countenance. "Oh, lovely, lovely," she said. I asked, "What is lovely?" "What I see," she replied in low intense tones. "What do I see? Lovely brightness— wonderful beings." It is difficult to describe the sense of reality conveyed by her intense absorption in the vision.
>
> Then—seeming to focus her attention more intently on one place for a moment—she exclaimed, almost with a kind of joyous cry, "Why, it's Father! It would be perfect if only W. [her husband] could come too."
>
> Her baby was brought for her to see. She looked at it with interest, and then said, "Do you think I ought to stay for the baby's sake?" Then turning toward the vision again, she said, "I can't—I can't stay; if you could see what I do, you would know I can't stay."
>
> But she turned to her husband, who had come in, and said, "You won't let the baby go to anyone who won't love him, will you?" Then she gently pushed him to one side saying, "Let me see the lovely brightness."

These individuals were able to see the world after this, and this sight removed all pain and fear and provided a measure of peace for them and their families.

The accounts of individuals who "died" and returned to life are equally informative. They invariably report that whatever pain they were experiencing disappeared when they died, only to be restored when they returned to life. Death was not traumatic, painful, frightening, or prolonged, although the dying process may have been. As one individual reported:

> One minute I was racked with tremendous pain [the result of being crushed in an automobile crash], the next I was out of my body and free of all pain. I don't know how I got out of the physical body, but as soon as I was free, all pain stopped. I found myself above the wreck. I could see my crumpled body and felt repulsed by it. When I was told (there were two beings with me) that I had to return to my body, I tried to argue with them. They reminded me of my obligations to my wife and two sons and that I had not yet completed the work I had agreed to do. I was torn. I did not want to return to that mangled body, but when they said that they would be with me, help me cope with the pain, I said, "OK." Almost before I had finished saying OK, than I was back in my body. The shock of the pain was excruciating and I immediately regretted my decision. The only thing that kept me going was the fact that I could feel their presences on really bad days and the knowledge that once my work was finished, they would be waiting for me.

Entering the World of Light

At the moment of death, most of those having an NDE are still in the physical world. They can see their physical body, its surroundings, and hear doctors, nurses, family, and friends, yet they are unable to communicate with them. One young medical student, George Ritchie, not knowing what else to do, tried to go home. Some look around themselves for cues as to what they should do. Some feel pulled by an unseen force. Others sense the presence of others who are there to assist them. Many individuals report that someone is there to serve as their guide or escort. Dr. Elisabeth Kübler-Ross says that what her patients feared most was being alone when they died. Based on her experience with thousands of dying people, she is able to assure her patients that they will not be alone when they die, that someone, usually a family member or a very close friend, will be awaiting their arrival with love and excitement.

While infants, young children, and adults share similar experiences as they enter the spirit world, there are some intriguing differences.

Infants. Some individuals who have had near-death experiences report seeing infants who have died. One of these was a woman who, in August of 1848, had an extensive visit to the world of spirits. While there she saw an angel carrying an infant in her arms. She commented:

> One [angel] drew near me. I saw in her arms an
> infant. "Whence came this?" I inquired; and the
> angel answered, "I received it from a heart-broken

mother at the gateway of death, as the spark of life expired in the external world, and I am conveying it to the sphere of infancy in the paradise of peace."

Her spirit guide also told her that specific angels have been assigned to protect infants and to "meet infant spirits as they leave the external world and enter into the spiritual." She then reported two children came toward her and she was told by one that children who die in infancy are innocent and are taken directly to paradise. The child went on to encourage her to tell parents that they were happy where they were and they were free from pain and sorrow. There they learned, lived in harmony, and were happy, and if parents could only realize the true condition of their dead infants, they would be happy. The woman was then taken to a place where all infants are gathered for instruction. That is where they arrive first and are nourished by their guardian angels. This is their home until they attain to a higher degree, where the instruction is adapted to a more advanced intellectual level.

Evidently infants who die are cared for, instructed, and grow. And when their parents' time comes to die, these children might well be the ones there to greet their parents, as happened with one mother. She had had twelve children die as infants. As she herself lay dying, she saw all twelve of her infant children in the room to welcome and accompany her into the next world.

Children. Children's experiences at death are similar to those of adults in that those they meet identify themselves as guardian angels. But, unlike adults, they often see other children with whom they converse and play. For example, twelve-

91

year-old Minnie Chatham, who died 1873, had a very fascinating experience.

> Shortly before she died, Minnie sat up in bed
> and said, "The angels have come for me, I must go!
> They are at the door waiting for me. Do, Ma, let
> me go!" And then she looked up toward heaven and
> continued. "Look at the little children! Oh, Ma, I
> must go!"

When ten-year-old Lillian Lee lay dying, she spoke to her
father and said she saw the golden gates open with crowds of
children coming out. They came up to her and kissed her and
called her by a different name. Then she whispered to the unseen children that she was coming.

Nine-year-old Katie, while unconscious at the bottom of a
swimming pool, does not remember drowning, but she does
remember this as related by Melvin Morse:

> A tunnel opened and through that tunnel came
> "Elizabeth." Elizabeth was "tall and nice" with
> bright golden hair. She accompanied Katie up the
> tunnel, where she saw her late grandfather and met
> several other people. Among her "new friends"
> were two young boys—souls waiting to be born—
> named Andy and Mark, who played with her and
> introduced her to many people.

Ann was a child of four with acute leukemia when she had
the following experience:

I noticed a light coming into the room. It was a beautiful golden-white light which seemed to appear in the wall to the left of my bed.

I sat up and watched the light grow. It grew rapidly in both size and brightness. In fact the light got so bright that it seemed to me that the whole world was lit by it. I could see someone inside the light. There was this beautiful woman, and she was part of the light: in fact she glowed.

I asked her who she was and she explained that she was my guardian and had been sent to take me to a place where I could rest in peace. The love emanating from her washed over me so that I didn't hesitate to put my hand in hers.

A nine-year-old boy dying from peritonitis saw and identified his grandmother, who had died eleven years before he was born.

As his mother held his hand, he said: "How small you are growing. Are you still holding my hand? Grandma is larger than you, isn't she? There she is. She is larger, isn't she. Her hand is larger than yours. She is holding one hand and her hand is larger than yours."

This young lad died with one hand being held by his mother, whom he was leaving, and the other held by his grandmother, whom he was joining. What a beautiful experience.

Adults. Adults, once they realize that they are dead, often discover they are in the presence of other beings. Some of these beings identify themselves as guides, escorts, or guardian angels, and many are deceased relatives or friends. In April 1928 William Dudley Pelley died and later reported what he experienced:

> I was whirling madly. Once in 1920 over San Francisco an airplane in which I was a passenger went into a tailspin and we almost fell into the Golden Gate. That feeling! Someone reached out, caught me, stopped me. A calm, clear, friendly voice said close to my ear:
>
> "Take it easy, old man. Don't be alarmed. You're all right. We're here to help you."
>
> Someone had hold of me, two persons in fact. One with a hand under the back of my neck, supporting my weight, the other with an arm under my knees. I was physically flaccid from my tumble.
>
> "Feeling better?" the taller of the two asked considerately, as physical strength to sit up unaided came to me and I took note of my surroundings.
>
> "Yes," I stammered. "Where am I?"
>
> They never answered my question. They did not need to answer my question. I knew what had happened. I had gone through all the sensations of dying. . . .
>
> I looked to the two friends who had received me. There were no other persons anywhere in evidence in the first half of my experience.

Somehow I knew those two men—knew them intimately as I knew the reflection of my own features in a mirror. And yet something about them, their virility, their physical "glow," their strong and friendly personality sublimated, as it were, kept me from instant identification.

The next account occurred in the 1890s, when a dying woman was met by her entire family, who had gathered to meet and greet her.

A short time before her decease, her eyes being fixed on something that seemed to fill her with pleasant surprise, she exclaimed: "Why! There is sister Charlotte here; and Mother and Father, and brother John and sister Mary! And now they have brought Bessy Heap! They are all here. Oh! How beautiful; how beautiful! Cannot you see them? Why they are all here, and they are come to bear me away with them. Part of our family have crossed the flood, and soon the other part will be gathered home, and then we shall be a family complete in heaven."

In a second case, a woman saw her father and sister (who had died in 1896 and 1898, respectively).

I saw them both sitting together at a small table, and it was spread with a spotless white cloth. They were not speaking, but looked perfectly happy and so contented. I put my face between the two and said, "What are you waiting for?"

My sister looked up with the sweetest smile, and said, "We are waiting for you." I said, "Are you happy here?" She looked up again and said, "Oh, so happy!"

The function of guardian angels seems to be to ease the transition from the physical world to the next. Depending on the nature of the condition that projected them into the next world, the reaction of the individual and their spirit companions varied significantly. Those who were forced out of this world through sudden, traumatic, and unexpected circumstances often expressed an initial confusion of what had happened to them and where they were. Such individuals found themselves observing, as interested spectators, scenes unfolding before them. Apparently the primary role of the guardian angel, in these circumstances, is to help them realize what has happened, to assure them that they are not alone, and to help guide them to their new home. Or, as will be discussed later, to introduce them to family, friends, and other beings who have preceded them into the World of Light and, if necessary, to return them to their physical bodies.

Bill, a forty-two-year-old ex-marine, had an NDE as a result of an all-terrain vehicle accident. In his case, he was not certain what was happening to him.

As I walked along the path in the meadow I came to a stone archway. It seemed almost as if I were called, or drawn, to the archway. I walked through it and entered a courtyard where I saw my father. He was dressed all in white, and he was bathed in sort of an iridescent white light.

We approached each other, and I remember telling him that I was feeling lost and confused. I realized at that point that I was either in the process of dying, or I had already died. My confusion centered on my earthly life. I was feeling a great loss because of my children, and I was sharing that feeling with my father.

My father said to me: "You aren't going to be lost or confused any longer. Everything will be fine. It's not time for you to be here, now, but when it is I will be here." Then he embraced me—there was an enormous outpouring of peace—and he took me back to the archway. As I entered the archway, I had the feeling that everything would be okay.

For those whose deaths are due to protracted illness, it is apparently the duty of the guardian angel to let them know that their death is near so they can prepare their families and complete any unfinished business and also to let them know that someone is waiting to greet and escort them.

In the following account a seventeen-year-old girl saw her escort—and so did her attending nurse! This account was cited by Sir William Barrett in his collection of deathbed visions and is included here in an abbreviated form.

It was about six months after I began to work in the hospital that it was revealed to me that the dying often do see those who have come from the

realms of spirit life to welcome them on their entrance into another state of existence.

Laura Stirman, a sweet girl of seventeen was a
personal friend of mine. She was a victim of con-
sumption. She suffered no pain, but the weariness
that comes from extreme weakness and debility was
heavy upon her and she yearned for rest.

A short time before she expired I became aware
that two spirit forms were standing by the bedside,
one on either side of it. I did not see them enter the
room; they were standing by the bedside when they
first became visible to me. . . . I recognized their
faces as those of two girls who had been the closest friends of the girl who was dying. They had
passed away a year before and were then about her
own age. . . .

[She] recognized them immediately. A smile,
beautiful to see, lit up her face. She stretched forth
her hands and in joyous tones exclaimed, "Oh, you
have come to take me away! I am glad, for I am very
tired."

As she stretched forth her hands the two angels
each extended a hand, one grasping the dying girl's
right hand, the other her left hand. Their faces were
illuminated by a smile more radiantly beautiful even
than that of the face of the girl who was so soon to
find the rest for which she longed. She did not
speak again but for nearly a minute her hands remained outstretched, grasped by the hands of the
angels, and she continued to gaze at them with glad
light in her eyes and the smile on her face.

The angels seemed to relax their grasp of the girl's hands, which then fell back on the bed. A sigh came from her lips, such as one might give who resigns himself gladly to a much-needed sleep, and in another moment she was what the world calls dead. But that sweet smile with which she had first recognized the angels was still stamped on her features.

The two angels remained by the bedside during the brief space that elapsed before the spirit form took shape above the body in which physical life had ceased. Then they arose and stood for a few moments one on each side of her, who was now like unto themselves; and three angels went from the room where a short time before there had been only two.

It is comforting to know that loving friends, relatives, or special emissaries will be there to guide or escort those who die. It is also comforting to know that those who die are greeted by beings who love them unconditionally, as was reported by Marshall Gibson, who experienced a massive heart attack in 1922.

There was a feeling of love and peace. On earth there always seems to be something . . . you know how things always bother you here. There's always some problem troubling you—either it's health, or money, or people, or war—or something. That was missing there. I felt completely at peace, as if there were no problems which were of concern. It wasn't that there were no challenges. It's just that every-thing seemed to be under control. It was such a wonderful feeling that I never wanted to lose it.

Summary

Death is not a painful experience, but one of peace and seren-ity. Infants, young children, and adults have similar experi-ences as they enter the spirit world. However, infants who die are met by specific angels who protect infants. They are cared for and instructed until they reach a more advanced youthful existence. Children's experiences at death are similar to those of adults, but they often see other children with whom they can converse and play. Adults are met by guides, escorts, or guardian angels that may be deceased relatives or friends. Their function seems to be to ease them through the transi-tion from the physical world to the next world.

CHAPTER 7

The Nature of
the Spirit Body

Just what is it that survives death? It is evident from the accounts reported in chapter 6 that those who die retain an identifiable and familiar identity. They are seen and have bodies that resemble those they had on earth. But just how much of "them" is carried over into the next life? This chapter examines the accounts of those who were permitted to see into the spirit world as they were dying and the reports of those who "died" and were permitted or required to return to life.

The first account is that of an off-duty policeman who found himself among a group of people standing around a car involved in an accident, where a girl was busy pulling a body out of the car. He finally was able to see the face of the body being pulled from the car and was shocked to see it was his own. After the girl began to give his body mouth-to-mouth resuscitation, he saw nothing more until he gained consciousness in the hospital.

As noted in the previous chapter, one's death may be the result of some very traumatic event, but death itself is neither painful nor traumatic. This man was not even aware that he had died. When he got close enough to see the face of the victim, he was startled and amazed to see it was his body the woman was trying to revive.

Theresa also did not realize that she was no longer alive after experiencing a major heart attack. During her attack she was racked with pain, when suddenly all her pain disappeared.

> I felt terrific. All pain left me and I felt light— as if I had lost fifty pounds. It was wonderful. My surroundings were black and I didn't see anything, but I felt terrific.

Why she felt so terrific was not clear to her until she met her cousin.

> In the blackness I saw a light—originally it was a small light. The light penetrated the blackness, and it was soft.
>
> In the light was my cousin who had shot himself earlier. He looked wonderful, and the full beard that he had on earth was gone—he was clean shaven. Drawing near to me, the light got brighter, and I could feel my cousin's love embrace me. When he moved closer to me he didn't walk; he sort of floated.
>
> I was overjoyed at seeing him, and I asked him how he was doing. He gently turned me around, and I saw someone lying on a bed. Looking down on the person in the bed, I saw all the machines and

tubes that were attached to the person. Feeling compassion for whoever was lying there, I wondered who it was.

Looking again at my cousin, I said: "What are you doing here Allen?" He responded with: "You should ask yourself that question." My thoughts were, What a stupid thing to say to me. What's going on here?

Allen gave me a strange look as to say: "You still don't get it, do you?" He didn't come right out and tell me what was happening. It was more as if I were supposed to figure it out.

As I pondered what was going on, I felt Allen's hand come up behind me and press, firmly but gently, on the back of my head. He then pushed me until my face was very close to the body in the bed. Staring directly into the face of the person in the bed, the light finally came on, and I thought, oh my heck, that's me.

I'm not sure why, but it was very hard for me to recognize myself. When I did, I felt sad . . . so very sad, so sorry for myself.

Looking at Allen, I said: "That's me." And he assured me that it was. Still wondering about Allen, though, I asked him why he was there. "Aren't you dead?" I asked him, and he said, "Yes." "Then I must be dead, also," I said. Allen responded with, "Bingo."

Apparently everyone does not instantly realize that they have died. Earthly concerns, desires, expectations, and habits do not suddenly cease with death, and as in Theresa's situation it took her cousin to help her to realize that she was dead.

It took George Ritchie, a young soldier training to become a physician during World War II, a long time to realize that he had died. His first memories of his unusual experience occurred when he awoke. He sat up in his bed and found himself in a tiny room. He got out of bed, noticed that there was someone in the bed, but didn't realize it was him. He left the room to find an orderly, and when he did, the orderly refused to acknowledge his presence or to answer his questions. When he tried to force the orderly to respond to him, he was shocked when his hand and arm went through the orderly. Puzzled by this experience, but not suspecting that he had died, he left the tent and headed toward his home in Virginia. As he traveled he found himself rising higher and higher until he was looking down on West Texas towns flashing below him (which he told himself was impossible). He decided to return to Camp Barkley, Texas, to try to find out what was happening to him. When he arrived, he searched until he found the tiny room with the person still in bed. The person's hand was hanging below the covers, and he was shocked to see his class ring on the hand and that the hand had to be his. He observed:

> But . . . if that was my ring, then—then it was me lying under that sheet. Did it mean that I was . . . It was the first time in this entire experience that the word "death" occurred to me in connection with what was happening.
>
> But I wasn't dead! How could I be dead and still be awake? Thinking. Experiencing.

Ritchie's question suggests that he believed that with death comes a cessation of the activities associated with the physical body, including action and thought. Obviously that was not what he was experiencing, and this shocked him. He had a body with legs, hands, and feet. He could not only hear and see, he could think and act. He had a body not too different from his physical body in appearance and function but significantly different in other ways. But what he could not do was be seen or communicate with the living.

The Spiritual Body

Appearance. Vern Swanson, during his experience, was visited by his deceased wife, Elaine. What he saw both surprised and delighted him.

> One night, about six months after Elaine and our son died, I was lying restlessly in bed. Suddenly I looked up and I saw a light. Standing there in the light was my wife.
>
> As I remember, it seems as if I were instantly out of bed—and next to her. It was the most interesting situation you could imagine, because she looked exactly like Elaine, yet she didn't. It's hard to explain.
>
> My wife, the woman, the angel, in front of me was so peaceful, so beautiful. There was a light that came from within her so she glowed. It wasn't reflected light; it was almost as if there were a bright candle inside of her.

I had always thought that Grace Kelly, the movie star, was the most beautiful woman in the world. Elaine, standing before me, would have put Grace Kelly to shame. She was very white with that inner glow, and she was absolutely the most beautiful person I had ever seen. To this day I can remember how she looked, and I marvel at what I saw. Elaine, in life, was a good-looking woman, working as a model during college, but her earthly body was a poor shadow, an impoverished copy, when compared with that beautiful person before me—yet it was Elaine.

Vern's experience left him with a sense of peace and hope. His wife, Elaine, was still alive; he vividly saw that to be true. He also discovered that Elaine had a body, a visible body that resembled the one she'd had while alive on earth. In addition to Vern's report, many NDEs have been recorded that reveal similar and additional information on what the "spirit" body is like.

In the following account, the reactions of Herman Stulz to his out-of-body condition is typical of some individuals when they first realize that they are out of their physical body. This account was taken from his personal journal.

I saw a strange man who was clothed in a robe, standing at the foot of my bed. He greeted me with a smile and invited me to come along with him. Instantly my spirit came out of my tortured body and stood before my bed; and I saw the nurse taking a pair of steel tweezers, reach down my throat and

106

pull up my tongue, which had slipped into the windpipe, causing the famous death rattle. I was released from all pain, soreness, and the burning sensation one feels after such an abdominal operation. I felt like I was never sick at all and filled with a glow of health I never felt before in my life.

But I wanted to make sure, whether this was only a dream, and to make sure I began to move my legs, my arms, and fingers. I grabbed my hair, pulled my ears, and began to walk around the room, and everything functioned like it did in mortality.

I thought this must be the death feared by all men. But for me, it was a feeling of ecstasy. I felt so light, like a newborn man. All my limbs worked with ease almost to perfection. I was really dead. . . .

I was a dual personality; on the bed lay my dead body of flesh and bones absolutely lifeless and dead. But my spirit in the same image stood before that bed, freed from all pains filled with new life and ambitions and new hope to live. Now I understood that it is the spirit that gives the power to the mortal body of flesh and bones to function and keep alive.

Peter E. Johnson, who was stricken with malaria in 1898, described the spirit body succinctly:

My spirit left the body; just how I cannot tell. But I perceived myself standing four or five feet in the air, and saw my body lying on the bed. I felt perfectly natural, but as this was a new condition I began to make observations. I turned my head, shrugged my shoulders, felt with my hands, and realized that it was I myself. I also knew that my body was lying lifeless, on the bed. While I was in a new environment, it did not seem strange, for I realized everything that was going on, and perceived that I was the same in the spirit as I had been in the body.

Alice Becker was also surprised to see her body. She noted that "she had somehow become detached and was looking down at her dead body. . . . To her she felt perfectly normal, almost like she still had her body."

Raymond Moody spoke to a man who had studied the hands of his spirit body. He told Raymond that his hands were composed of light with tiny structures in them. He could even see the delicate whorls of his fingerprints.

Theresa, the woman mentioned earlier in this chapter, also noticed that a light was emanating from her body.

Looking at my hands I could see that they were white and they glowed—and I was dressed in a glowing white garment. I could feel the energy coming from me. It was coming from every part of my body.

A second man, like Stulz, checked out his spirit body.

To find out whether I had substance, I rubbed my hands together and I felt my face with my hands. In both cases I found that I had form and substance. I could feel myself. Looking at my

hands, I saw that they looked like my hands normally did, except there was a glow to them. These
discoveries excited me. I remember thinking: Wow,
this is great.

Others have remarked on the features of the spirit bodies
of others they met while out of their physical bodies.

It's hard to describe, but somehow the spirit
body combined the youth and vigor of twenty-one-
year-olds, with a sense of perfect maturity.

All their faces looked fresh, like the faces of very
healthy people who are out of doors all the time.

It also seemed that the longer a being was in any
of these realms [spirit world], the closer they came
in appearance to being around 30 to 35 years of
age.

These observations of those who met others during their
experience suggest that the longer a being was in the spirit
world, the closer they came in appearance to what they would
have looked like around thirty to thirty-five years of age. For
example, following are the accounts of three individuals who
noted specifically that the ravages of old age had been reversed and that those they saw were happy, healthy, and in the
prime of life.

And there in the doorway of this beautiful city
stood my mother who'd died 50 years before, her

arms open wide to receive me. All the lines of age had slipped from her face. She looked like a very young woman. There was no pain on her face as there'd been when I'd last seen her.

My grandmother had been ninety-six.... she looked perhaps 40 or 45. My mother was 60 when she died and way over weight, and she looked trim and a good general health look, happy and healthy.

Looking toward the light, I saw my wonderful great-grandmother, the one who had helped raise me, and the one who offered me most of the love that I got as a child. She had died about seven years before that, and she was more beautiful than I remembered her. She was dressed in a soft white-flowing material. There were no shadows in her face, and she appeared to be about thirty years of age. I remembered her as an old woman.

Unlike the physical body, the spirit body lacks the disabilities and limitations that formerly plagued the physical body, as evidenced by the following three accounts.

I saw two figures walking toward me and I immediately recognized them. They were my mother and father, both had died years ago. My mother was an amputee and yet that leg was now restored! She was walking on two legs.

Then she said she saw her dead husband Ben, who had lost a leg and eye in the Civil War. "There is Ben," she said. "And he has both of his eyes and both of his legs!"

In the next account a man noted that his transition was serene and peaceful. He found himself walking up a beautiful green hill.

> The transition was serene and peaceful. I was walking up a beautiful green hill. It was steep, but my leg motion was effortless and a deep ecstasy flooded my body. Despite three incisions in my body from operations, I stood erect without pain, enjoying my tallness, free from inhibitions about it.

In the last account, an individual observed that

> approaching me from the front, and I recognized them immediately, were my grandparents. They approached me. I knew that it was them, but they weren't old as my grandparents had been. They walked very upright, with no arthritis, and with no wrinkles. . . .

On October 22, 1976, Elane Durham had an extensive NDE, during which she found herself in an indescribably beautiful place.

> I was dressed in a long white flowing gown. The whiteness in the gown was different from any white I had seen before; there were depth and iridescence associated with it. It was an alive white, as were all

111

the other colors. It was a pure white, and it was as if you could see into its depth and glowing beauty. My hair was long, unlike what it was in life.

I ran across the grass, and my feet didn't touch the ground. I could feel the air around me—not that there was a lot of wind—just a refreshing feeling of the air.

In the distance by the river there were six or seven people standing by some trees, and I could tell they were waiting for me. It was as if they knew I was coming; one of them looked up and said: "There she is!" A man leaning against a tree motioned with his arm and said, "Hurry, Elane, everyone's waiting."

Running toward them, I felt the air against me, but my feet didn't touch the ground. Power and energy were coming off everything. I realized that everything there had a life and personality to it.

Two women broke away from the group and began running toward me. When they got within about twenty feet, I recognized one as my grandmother. She had been dead since I was about nine years old. The man against the tree was my mother's step-dad, and he had been dead since I was sixteen or seventeen. The lady immediately behind my grandmother was Aunt Virginia, my husband's aunt, who had died the previous February.

All of them were dressed in white, a white which radiated light. Their hair and faces were not the same as on earth, but I recognized them quickly. They were about thirty years of age in appearance, much younger than when I had seen them last. Aunt Virginia was badly crippled when I knew her in life with one leg shorter than the other. Here, she was completely restored to normal function.

As I saw my relatives and felt of their joy, I had the thought: Man, if my kids could only see this; if they could only see Aunt Virginia now. I no sooner had the thought than: WHAM. It was a heavy duty body slam, and I was back in my body at the hospital.

Because of genetic factors or nutritional problems, some individuals may be shorter in life than they could have been. In such a case, one's spirit body would logically be larger than the physical body. Consider the following:

> Then I discovered that I had become larger than in earth life, and congratulated myself. I am somewhat smaller in body than I like to be, but in the next life, I am to be as I desire.

The person who dies has a perfect as well as whole spiritual body, as demonstrated by the NDE account of a man who lost part of his leg in an accident that resulted in his clinical death. He felt his body during his NDE and it was whole.

In another NDE account, Joy Melvin went to the otherworld, where she saw her deceased relatives, including her brother, who lost his legs in a car accident. She ran up to her brother in the otherworld and ran her hands down his body. He lifted her up and said: "I'm whole here, Joy, I'm whole here."

* * *

Other individuals who were affected with genetic problems that resulted in mental and physical handicaps were no longer handicapped. Vicky, a blind twelve-year-old girl, had her NDE in 1963 as the result of peritonitis. During her experience, she was able to see for the first time in her life, an experience that surprised, delighted, and confused her. She also met two deceased friends, Debby and Diane. Vicky had met these two girls while she was a student at a school for the blind. She had grown very close to Debby. Debby was a hydrocephalic and received a lot of ridicule from the other students because she was slow and had a severe breathing problem. Because she befriended Debby a lot of people made fun of her as well. Debby was the first person Vicky met during her experience. As soon as they saw each other, Debby came toward her to hug her. Right behind Debby she saw Diane, another blind handicapped friend she had known at the school. Diane had drowned at age six during a seizure. Vicky reported that she did not know what they looked like, but she had hugged Debby and knew that she was very overweight. But when she saw them they were beautiful. They were more mature, older, than they were in real life. Debby was perfected. She was brilliant. Her face was light, bright, and happy. Neither girl was fat, slow, or disabled in any way. They had been healed and were beautiful.

The ravages of debilitating disease do not affect the spiritual body, as George discovered. George fell asleep at the wheel of his car and was "killed" when he ran into a bridge abutment. The first thing he remembered was standing in front of a person he recognized as his good friend Tom, who had died five years earlier. When they met, Tom was twenty-one and completely bald, a side effect of the diabetes that would ultimately kill him. The first thing that Tom said to George was that he had to go back because it was not his time. George noted that Tom, who had been bald and thin when he was alive, had a full head of dark curly hair.

New Abilities. A woman reflecting on her NDE noted that her "new" body not only retained the senses of the physical body, but had additional senses.

> When I went into the garden I was in a different body than the one I had left. I was not overweight, I was maybe even on the thin side. I seemed to be a young woman; not adolescent, but not the 35 years old that I was at the time. I had long black hair and my body was perfect. Just as beautiful as it could be. And I had more senses than the five senses we have on this earth. I had more perception.

A second individual elaborated on his newly acquired senses.

> It was like I had increased awareness. On earth our body has five senses, but over there I had more than the five senses. Part of the expanded awareness was the ability to perceive thoughts, to peer into the souls of all living things, and to communicate with them.

Others reported the law of gravitation had no hold upon them; they could move about without the slightest effort and with great rapidity. Also, they were aware of pure knowledge; they could understand many things. One person discovered he had tremendous mental agility and, in addition, was able to see in every direction at the same time. A man recorded in his account that his vision was incredibly more powerful, and one woman recalled that her senses had no limitations—she could look anywhere and everywhere.

Sight. Of the five senses, hearing and sight are the ones most commonly mentioned by individuals who have had an NDE. A woman blinded by complications associated with acute multiple sclerosis had this experience:

> DeAnne awoke, and although unable to see, she began crying. When asked why she was crying DeAnne explained that she had just had a gorgeous experience and she didn't want it to quit. She told the doctor and Fred [her husband] that she had been in this beautiful place, with brightness all around, where she could see again, and where there was no anguish or pain. She met her father there, who had previously died, and he looked wonderful. He was wearing a long white robe and he was not wrinkled as she remembered him in life. He told her that he was thrilled she didn't have to suffer so much anymore.
>
> After seeing her father she became aware that she had to return. She awoke to find that she was back in the hospital, blind again, and in terrible pain. That was why she was crying.

In a second case, a seventy-year-old woman, who had been blind since the age of eighteen had a heart attack and "died." After she was resuscitated she not only described the instruments her physicians used to revive her, but she could even describe their colors. The most amazing thing about this was that most of these instruments weren't even thought of over fifty years ago when she could last see. On top of all this, she was even able to tell the doctor that he was wearing a blue suit at the time of her resuscitation.

In the preceding two cases, individuals who had become blind were delighted to have their sight restored, if only for a short time. In the next case, Vicky, a young woman blind since birth, saw for the first time.

The first thing she was aware of was that she was near the ceiling. She heard a doctor talking and looked down. At first she was startled that she could see. She was shocked and totally in awe. She could not even describe being able to see. She said it was much better than she ever imagined.

She then reported that she went up through the roof of the hospital. She could see light, the streets below her, and buildings. When she was asked about color, she said she did not know what colors were. But what she did see were various shades of brightness. She speculated that the different intensity of lights she saw might be what sighted people meant by color. She had never before seen light, never been taught what color meant, and hence could not interpret anything she saw by color. She said that when she first saw, she found it confusing and disorienting and even somewhat scary, frightening, and overwhelming. But once she was in the presence of the "light" she had no question that she could see, and sight was fantastically beautiful.

Susan Burt, who died from complications accompanying the birth of her twins, reported, "while she was out of her body, she enjoyed 360 degree vision, and she had no pain."

Hearing. At the moment of death, many individuals report hearing doctors or others pronounce them dead. However, once they meet spirit beings, they report that communication is not through voice but mind to mind. They know what the other person is thinking, so spoken communication is unnecessary. This might seem to indicate that hearing is a physical attribute and unnecessary in the spirit world. Consider, however, the following two experiences:

> I don't know how I got there, but I found myself in a beautiful country lane. I was strolling down the lane slowly and I felt I had all the time in the world. I could hear the Sky Larks singing and I thought "Oh, how lovely."

> I could hear, as I had never heard in my life before. I could hear the soft whisper of winds in the trees below me. I could hear the ripple and tinkle of many running waters. I could hear the distant shouts of children at play, and the joyous barking of a dog. I could hear the singing of many birds in the trees below. I had not heard the singing of birds for many years.

Other individuals report hearing bells ringing, birds singing, brooks running, children playing, and the wind in the trees during their experience. Many individuals report hearing heavenly music, including choirs and singing children. For some the capacity to hear was so enhanced that they could actually hear the sounds of flowers blooming and grass growing.

Smell. Various individuals report that it is impossible to describe the fragrant aromas of the flowers, trees, and grasses of the next world, where their delicate perfumes fill the air. Herr Pettersson was accompanied by a guardian angel in his trip into the spirit world:

> Presently they came to a park in which there were all kinds of beautiful trees bearing inviting fruit; also flowers that delighted the eye and filled the air with fragrance.

A second man who reported that he had died on the operating table found himself in the most beautiful park he had ever seen. He saw the trees in full bloom and the sun shining. He smelled the flowers and heard the birds and a trickling brook.

Kenneth lapsed into a coma on his way to the racetrack and died later that day in the intensive care unit of the hospital. Upon recovery, he reported a very fascinating account of his visit to the other side. He reported among many other things that "I could smell the forest and the grasses and the flowers. Everything smelled fresh. It was very pleasant and not overpowering."

General William Booth reported that all of the earth's sweetest floral extracts are only poor imitations of the heavenly perfumes he experienced on the other side.

✣   ✣   ✣

Touch. The sense of touch is very much a part of the new spirit body. For example, a child reported that he saw children and that they ran up to him and kissed him. A second child reported that a man held him and it felt so good that he wanted to stay but was told no. A thirty-eight-year-old woman saw a deer, which she felt lick her face. A young boy met a deceased pet that licked his face and hand. A four-year-old boy told his parents that he felt a warm hand on his shoulder. A man met two individuals who knew his name and shook hands with him. One woman felt soft breezes and another the grass on the bottoms of her feet. A young woman was hugged by her deceased cousins.

Taste. General Booth reported that while he was in the spirit world, he could pick and taste the fruit, which he described as beyond all earthly sweetness. Rebecca Springer said that she had eaten a fruit resembling a Bartlett pear, but much larger and much more delicious. Another man had delicious fruit set before him.

One man who had just arrived in the world of spirits felt very hungry and asked his wife who had preceded him:

> "Does one eat here?"
> She replied, "Oh—yes, if you want to. You can have anything you wish."
> And then there appeared on the table before me just the meal I had in my mind. I ate it with very great enjoyment.
> But I noticed that she only toyed with her food.

120

"You are not hungry," I said.

"Well, you see—when we first come over the desire for food is still strong in us, and we would not be happy unless we could satisfy it. But the longer we are here the less we want."

Evidently food is not required by the spirit body for survival, but it exists for the pleasure of taste and to help new arrivals to adjust.

Breathing. Breathing is not one of the five senses, but De-Lynn, a forty-two-year-old man afflicted with cystic fibrosis, was ecstatic that he could breathe for the first time in his life without pain.

One amazing aspect of my experience attracted my attention. Because I had suffered from cystic fibrosis since youth I was not aware that breathing could be a pleasant exercise. I soon noticed, in the tunnel, that I was breathing and it didn't hurt. I could actually fill my lungs and it didn't burn, it didn't sting, it didn't tickle. How exhilarating it was for someone who had never breathed without difficulty. Filling my lungs was such a pleasure that I stayed in the same place for a moment simply enjoying it.

Not only were my lungs responding without pain, I next noticed that I had no pain throughout my body. Pain had been a constant companion throughout my life. I had learned to accept it as normal. I learned there, however, that pain was not normal. For the first time I realized how intense my pain had been. It was a wonderful feeling—to be without pain—one that I sometimes have to force myself to forget when I am having painful sieges in the hospital.

Emotions. Most people would expect that individuals would feel emotions such as joy, acceptance, kindliness, and love in the next world. While these heavenly emotions were experienced, so were other more earthly emotions such as humor, laughter, amusement, indignation, crying, and temper tantrums.

> Joan tried to kill herself when she was 27. She recalled screaming as she went into her NDE, "God, please let me know You forgive me before I die." From a bright light came two big hands, and then a loving, gentle voice, which took away all of Joan's fear, said, "Lift up your hands. I forgive you. I'll give you a second chance." Joan said God was love, compassion, kindness, total acceptance, and joy, and that He had a sense of humor and made her laugh. At one point during her NDE, she said, "I was silly, Lord," and He laughed.

A heart attack victim met his father, who had also died of a heart attack fifteen years before. "He hadn't changed a bit. We chatted quite naturally and he joked with me about my brothers."

A ten-year-old boy was crushed under a wall when it collapsed. Twice he was declared clinically dead by his doctor.

When he revived the second time he reported, "The second time I saw a great big city made of solid gold and filled with kids. They were so happy. We laughed together."

As the result of a heart attack, a man "died" and found himself in a rolling green meadow that was slightly uphill.

> I saw my brother and he was alive, and yet I remember when he had died. He was so glad to see me. We put arms around each other right there in the middle of the meadow. I had tears in my eyes and then we strolled arm in arm up the meadow.

A woman who had a severe allergic reaction to her anesthesia reported beings all around who acknowledged her presence. They totally accepted her and did not seem to mind that she was cranky and demanding to know where she was.

Following an automobile accident, a being told a woman that it was her turn to die and go to heaven. However, she argued with him and complained that she was too young to die and convinced him to allow her to live. About thirty years later, she had a cardiac arrest and found herself with the same being. This time she argued that she needed to raise her children and could not leave them. The being allowed her to return to life this second time but clearly informed her that the next time she died, she would have to stay in the spirit world.

In the previous two cases, individuals fought to live. In the next cases, young girls got very upset about having to return to their bodies. A nine-year-old girl did not want to return to her physical body and:

. . . was clutching the top rail of a rail fence. The last thing she wanted to do was to go back to her body. She heard them discussing her situation and they decided that she would have to go back. So, in her words, "I threw a tantrum. I pitched a royal fit. I grabbed on to the rail of the fence and wrapped my arms and legs around it and I wouldn't let go." The voice just laughed. "Look, you can have it later, but this is not the time. And throwing a tantrum is not going to do you any good."

Cynthia Prueitt was seven years old when she had her NDE.

The next thing I remember was being introduced into a room that was completely and brilliantly white. There was a man sitting on a chair that resembled a chair-type throne.

Seeing this man with a beard sitting there, I ran up to him and climbed on His knees. He gathered me in his arms and . . . He just began to comfort me. He gave me such a warm, warm feeling of love, and . . . I've never felt anything like it. It was warm, it was love, it was joy—I didn't want it to end. It was the most thrilling feeling I had ever experienced before or since.

This wonderful being wrapped me in His arms and held me close. I began to sob and tell Him my problems. He comforted me with words of comfort. Then He began to talk to me about my life. He told me that I had certain things in this life that

I had to do. He began to tell me what they were and how I was to accomplish these things. As He outlined what I was to do he asked me if I would try to accomplish what He had just described, and I promised that I would.

Then He said that it was time for me to leave. I began to bawl, and I told Him that I didn't want to go. Crying helplessly, I pled that I might stay in his presence. . . .

Evidently the God of anger, vengeance, and wrath is not the being that most people meet in the spirit world. Instead they meet a kind, gentle, loving being with a keen sense of humor, understanding, and infinite patience. It is also quite obvious that besides the five senses, individuals take with them their emotions, expectations, desires, and temperament. It takes time for many of them to adjust to the next life and to the new needs of the spirit body.

Not mentioned here, but included in a number of accounts, was the fact that addictive needs associated with alcohol, tobacco, and various drugs persist beyond the grave but cannot be assuaged there. It is also clear from many accounts that suicide will not resolve problems. Joan Forman, in summarizing information gleaned from those who had committed suicide, suggests that individuals who are now in the spirit world because they killed themselves discover that they have solved nothing. The same set of problems that drove them to the act is still present. Nevertheless, Ritchie is convinced by what he saw during his NDE that in spite of what they did, the Being of Light still loves and understands and will not "condemn them to hell."

Personal Identity

At death, one's personal identity does not change. The ravages of age, accidents, and ill health are removed, but not one's personality, attachments, personal interests, and desires. The reactions of a man when he realized he was dead and examined his new spirit body sums it up beautifully.

> I was totally me. Aside from the complete absence of pain and the total presence of peace (neither of which I had ever known on earth), I looked like me, reacted like me. I was me. I was the same size, the same shape, as the person I had seen in the mirror for years.

Summary

In the spirit world the individual has a spirit body. This spirit body resembles the body that a person has during life on earth. Evidently it is the life force for the physical body. The spirit body they discover lacks any disabilities and deformities that plagued the physical body. It is a new body, complete, perfect, with increased capabilities, and senses. The spirit body is in human form with head, arms, hands, legs, and so forth, has no restriction from the force of gravity, retains the senses and sensations of the mortal body, has increased capacities such as the ability to move with the speed of lightning, increased mental abilities, and increased power of sight, and appears to be at the age of young adulthood.

CHAPTER 8

The Location
of the Afterlife

Many of us have grown up with the idea that there is a heaven above with pearly gates and winged angels and a hell below with lakes of fire and brimstone. But these ideas are not confirmed by those who died and returned to life. Not only were their perceptions about the spirit body significantly altered by their experience, so were their ideas about the afterlife.

Tombstones often contain epitaphs and artwork that express the hope and belief that death is not the end of everything but that something continues beyond the grave. Images portraying a hope of life beyond the grave include the upraised arm with the finger pointing "heavenward," the bird and butterfly flying free in the heavens, the raised, tearstained faces looking expectantly toward the heavens. These images reflect the belief that heaven is somewhere away from the earth.

During medical crises and accidents individuals often find themselves elevated above their physical bodies, viewing the

scenes of their deaths, which would seem to support the belief that "heaven" is above and away from this earth. Also,
when the individuals leave the vicinity of their bodies, they
seem to rise up, often through some dark, tunnel-like void.
Many individuals report traveling very rapidly for a period of
time toward a light that becomes brighter and brighter. As
discussed in the previous chapter, it takes time for the spirit
body to free itself from the limitations of sensations and perceptions associated with the physical body. In other words,
what they see and hear is affected by the mind-set of the limited physical body. But time and space are physical facts that
do not seem to exist in the next world. So exactly how far they
went and where they went in relation to the physical earth is
unknown. Did they go light-years? Or did they just pass into
a different dimension? The only thing consistently reported
was that their passage took them through something.

Those who have made the trip have given us many clues
about the location and internal divisions of the otherworld.
For example, Daisy Irene Dryden was born in Marysville,
California, on September 9, 1854, and died in San Jose, California, on October 8, 1864, aged ten years and twenty-nine
days. In the summer of 1864 she was attacked by a "bilious
fever." During the last three days of her life she lingered on
the borderland of this world and the next.

Two days before she left us, the Sunday School
superintendent came to see her. She [Daisy] talked
very freely about going, and sent a message by him
to the Sunday School. When he was about to leave,
he said, "Well, Daisy, you will soon be over the
'dark river.'" After he had gone, she asked her father

what he meant by the "dark river." He tried to explain it, but she said: "It is all a mistake; there is no river; there is no curtain; there is not even a line that separates this life from the other life." And she stretched out her little hands from the bed, and with a gesture said, "It is here and it is there; I know it is so, for I can see you all, and I see them there at the same time."

When asked if she saw a heavenly city, she said, "I do not see a city," and a puzzled look came over her face, and she said, "I do not know; I may have to go there first." When asked by her mother, "How do you see the angels?" She replied, "I do not see them all the time; but when I do, the walls seem to go away, and I can see ever so far, and you couldn't begin to count the people; some are near, and I know them; others I have never seen before."

Once when her mother was sitting by her bedside, her hand clasped with Daisy. Looking up so wistfully she said, "Dear Mamma, I do wish you could see Allie; he is standing beside you." Involuntarily she looked around, but Daisy continued, "He says you cannot see him, because your spirit-eyes are closed, but that I can, because my body only holds my spirit, as it were, by a thread of life."

What is interesting about this account is that the description Daisy gave of her experience did not correspond with her preconceived ideas of the spirit world, yet it did not once occur to her to doubt what she was learning of a life apart from a physical body and the possession of a spiritual body because of her childlike trust in her brother who had died six months earlier and was her primary contact on the other side. Melvin Morse, in his book *Closer to the Light,* noted that children are less likely to question the reality of their NDE and therefore are more likely to experience the "light."

Daisy's account would suggest that the otherworld exists in the same place as the physical world but in a different dimension, and that to see it, in her words, your "spirit eyes" must be opened.

These experiences, incidentally, are not limited to children. In one account, the "spirit eyes" of a dying man were opened and he saw and greeted some thirty or forty friends and relatives who were waiting for him in the otherworld while simultaneously talking to his wife, who was at his bedside. One of those he greeted was the best man at his wedding, who unbeknownst to him had died two weeks before.

It is not unusual for the dying to be conversing with people from both sides of life and to express surprise at seeing specific persons they thought were alive but were on the other side. For example, the sister of a dying woman reported seeing many deceased relatives, including Ruth, who had died suddenly the previous week. When the dying woman saw Ruth she asked what she was doing there, and then she murmured a few last words.

These accounts are representative of numerous accounts that suggest that the world of the spirits and the living are very near—but in different dimensions. George Ritchie in his NDE observed a city superimposed on our physical city. He also noticed that the beings of one city were not aware of the existence of the other.

A very similar phenomenon was reported by Renee

Zamora, who died from an improperly diagnosed illness. She reported leaving her body and

> floating through the hospital wall . . . and suddenly . . . to a park. I remember wondering, 'What happened to the city?' As the thought entered my mind, I seemed to understand that the park was somehow overlaid upon the city, but slightly above it.

Jack Ausman was told by an angelic figure during his NDE that people are very near to those of the heavenly kingdom.

According to Daisy and her little brother, the reason the beings of both realms are unaware of the presence of those in the other is that our "spirit-eyes" have to be opened in order to see the spirit world, and once our "earth-eyes" become closed we are no longer aware of the physical world. This observation of Daisy's is supported by reports of individuals who visited the other side and were sought out by individuals there and asked about relatives and conditions on earth. For example, a young man was met by his father, who "wanted to know how Mother and Ed and Pren were, how Susie and Kate and Augusta were, and whether I had suffered much or been afraid. . . ."

Ella Jensen was also questioned by various individuals about their friends and relatives on earth. One of these individuals was her cousin. He asked her how his folks were getting along. He said that it grieved him to hear that some of his sons were using tobacco, liquor, and many other things that were injurious to them.

It might be assumed that those on the other side "know"

when deaths occur or when people are about to die. However, this may not always be the case, as evidenced by the surprise of Ella's grandfather at seeing her, and that some family members were not "ready" for her when she arrived. Many of these "unexpected" arrivals were sent back to finish their work on earth.

Divisions in the Otherworld

Information gleaned from individuals who have visited or been permitted to see the next world suggest that this otherworld has two major divisions. The first division has been named "Cities of Light" by Raymond Moody, Betty Eadie, Melvin Morse, and others. The other division has been variously labeled "a realm of bewildered spirits" by Moody, a place "devoid of love" by George Ritchie, a place of "earthbound/lingering spirits" by Eadie, and the "sphere of wasted, elusive, and misused opportunities" by Joy Snell. This division will be described in chapter 14.

Individuals who have had an extensive visit to the otherworld report that its structure is very complex. In the previous chapter it was noted that individuals acquired new senses in the spirit world, one of which is the ability to "know" others' thoughts and desires. This enhanced sense seems to be a factor in the ultimate placement of each individual in the spirit world.

There is evidence that a type of judgment occurs at the time of death. This judgment involves a review of a person's life and results in their placement in the spirit world. Many have told about an incredibly vivid, full-color, three-dimensional, instantaneous, panoramic review of every single thing they have ever done, thought, or said in their lives. In this review people see not only every action they have ever done, but also the effects of these actions upon others. In a number of cases the individual also experienced the emotions (both the pleasant and painful) that their actions caused. The person is aware that all of those present at the review also "see" their lives and the effects their acts had on the lives of others. Everyone knows the innermost thoughts, desires, and dreams of everybody else. There are no secrets. Hypocrisy is impossible because others know your thoughts the minute you think them.

Upon completion of the review, each individual knows where he or she belongs. The judgment that occurs during the life review is a judgment that comes from within. No court, judge, or jury is required. Each person knows exactly where he or she stands with the "Being of Light" and all others in the "City of Light."

One description of the life review was given by a twenty-nine-year-old woman who said:

> And then I experienced a replay of all my life and I'd love to know if other people have it. That was the most shocking thing of the whole experience, from my birth to the actual operation. I actually felt the operation. And it was like it was on fast forward video. I didn't even know about videos at the time but I know in recalling it. And it was through everything, every single thing that had ever happened. It was just the most amazing experience. And people, places, everything. I re-experienced my whole life.

133

Another example of the life review was recorded by Raymond Moody in 1977.

I first was out of my body, above the building, and I could see my body lying there. Then I became aware of the light—just light—being all around me. Then it seemed there was a display all around me, and everything in my life just went by for review, you might say. I was really very, very ashamed of a lot of things that I experienced because it seemed that I had a different knowledge, that the light was showing me what was wrong, what I did wrong. And it was very real.

It seemed like this flashback, or memory, or whatever was directed primarily at ascertaining the extent of my life. It was like there was a judgment being made and then, all of a sudden, the light became dimmer, and there was a conversation, not in words, but in thoughts. When I would see something, when I would experience a past event, it was like I was seeing it through eyes with (I guess you could say) omnipotent knowledge, guiding me, and helping me to see.

That's the part that has stuck with me, because it showed me not only what I had done but even how what I had done had affected other people. And it wasn't like I was looking at a movie projector because I could feel these things; there was feeling, . . . I found out that not even your thoughts are lost . . . Every thought was there.

A second report made nearly 130 years earlier by a man who drowned, reveals that nothing has changed but the reference to modern technology.

> ... traveling backwards, every incident of my past life seemed to me to glance across my recollection in retrograde progression; not, however, in mere outline as here stated, but the picture filled up, with every minute and collateral features; in short, the whole period of my existence seemed to be placed before me in a kind of panoramic review, and each act of it seemed to be accompanied by a consciousness of right or wrong, or by some reflection on its cause or consequences—indeed, many trifling events, which had long been forgotten, then crowded into my imagination, and with the character of recent familiarity.

In 1971 a woman underwent surgery for a persistent back condition. During it, her heart failed and she had an NDE while she was clinically dead for twenty minutes. She was shown her entire life by a spirit being of light. While she observed her life she experienced a self-judgment. She knew her sins had been forgiven but she could not forgive herself for some of the things she did and did not do in life. She discovered that it was the little things such as helping a hurt child or visiting a shut-in that matter most in life.

This description is typical and suggests that people know exactly where they belong in the other world. As one woman commented, "There was no voice of judgment, but I knew instantly how the Lord felt about each thing I had done in my life."

Sometime after the judgment the person is assigned (in many cases this assignment is self-imposed) to a specific place or level in the other world—a place where his or her spirit feels most at ease. Eadie "understood that there are many levels of development, and we always go to that level where we are most comfortable." This observation is supported by Barbara Ross, who "died" while being operated on after an automobile accident.

> My father looked just like he had looked the last time I saw him, pretty much in the prime of his life, calm and in control. Grandmother looked harassed and harried, kind of tense. I remember her being that way before she died. I got the feeling that she wasn't at as high a level of spiritual development as my father was. She had come from a different part of the afterworld, from a group of people who were unsettled as she was, less distinct in their appearance, and not as much in control as my father. He was benign and calm, like he had been in life.

Arthur Ford, after meeting many friends and relatives, wondered why some were missing. When asking about them, he began to experience less light and a haze, less brilliant colors, a heaviness of his body, and earthly thoughts. This impressed him to believe that he was being shown a lower sphere, where he saw those he asked about.

There is evidence of multiple levels in the otherworld. For example, one individual saw every man and woman in the otherworld organized into several different grades. Another individual discovered that

> there were spheres above, whose occupants could and did visit us, and we could always recognize these higher natures by the virtues which possessed them, and were apparent to us as they passed beside us. But we could not visit their spheres until we had perfectly qualified for it. . . .
> And there were of course spheres below us, where those who had not repented of their evil ways still had to work out their redemption. . . .
> Those in the lower spheres could not have been happy in this higher kingdom until they qualified themselves by a change of heart and mind.

This individual went on to observe that although individuals in each sphere are aware of the others' existence, they cannot see, let alone visit, without significant preparation.

> Those living on the higher planes of the city radiate the brightest light, being so resplendent that their glory must be cloaked so others of lower degree can look upon them. Visiting the higher levels is possible, but the spirits of lower realms must be prepared or covered so they can stand in the presence of greater glory.

In addition to the placement of individuals at judgment, the next world is efficiently organized to help individuals adapt to their new home. Infants are taken to a place where they are nurtured and taught and where they mature. Some new arrivals are taken to a place of orientation where they rest, adjust to their new condition, and prepare to take their place in the City of Light. Daisy Dryden, the young ten-year-old child mentioned earlier, had been conversing with her six-year-old brother, Allie, who had died of scarlet fever six months earlier. Daisy could not travel into the spirit world, but Allie could and would supply Daisy with some answers to specific questions. For example:

> Mrs. W., who had lost her father a short time previous, wanted to know if Daisy had seen him, and brought his picture to let her see if she could recognize him. Daisy told her she had not seen him and that Allie, whom she had asked about him (Mr. W.) had not seen him, but that Allie had said he would ask someone who could tell him about him. In a moment Daisy said, "Allie is here and says, 'Tell Aunty her father wants her to meet him in heaven, for he is there.'" Mrs. W. then said, "Daisy, why did not Allie know at once about my father?" "Because," replied she, "those who die go into different states or places and do not see each other at all times, but all the good are in the state of the blest."

Still others are being prepared to enter the City of Light.

> When told that a very close family friend—Dr. John Macgregor—was still working hard as a physician, the individual assumed he was working

138

with people on earth. "Oh, you're quite wrong," he said. "We have hospitals here full of injured and crippled souls—the result of their hard faring on earth—who need nursing back to health and building up into full stature before they can start their work up here."

Summary

The reports of many individuals who have been permitted to see or visit the next world tell us that it is located right here on our physical earth. If our spirit eyes were to open, we would discover we are surrounded by those who have preceded us in death. But not everyone goes to the same location in the next world. We will be acutely aware of everything we have done or failed to do in our lives. We will also know the lives of those around us and they will know ours. Therefore we will seek out those who "think" the same way we do, who "value" the same things we do. We will gravitate toward those we feel at ease with, who are like us. Judgment is more a process of self-evaluation than the product of a heavenly tribunal. The next world as will be documented later is segmented into spheres organized around qualities of love, service, and personal preparedness.

CHAPTER 9

Approaching the City of Light

Countryside Environment in the World of Light

Most of the reports of people who continue into the spirit world told of finding themselves in an incredibly beautiful place. Some stood awestruck by its splendor, while others walked about slowly, trying to understand and appreciate what they were seeing. They not only saw indescribable scenes of beauty, but also experienced a sense of peace and tranquillity.

One NDEr saw a gorgeous valley floor with foothills covered by uniform symmetrical trees that were tall and graceful without blemish. The valley had perfect and erect grasses interspersed with white, four-petaled flowers with gold centers on two-foot stems. He said there was nothing like it on earth.

Following is another description of the countryside.

I suddenly found myself in this beautiful place.
I was greeted by such warmth and happiness that it
was utter bliss. I was in a beautiful landscape, the

flowers, trees, the colours, were indescribable, not at all like the colours you see here. The peace and joy were overpowering. I felt warm and glowing. There was a blinding light, but it was not harsh and did not hurt my eyes. The beauty of the landscape is beyond description.

Landscape. The landscape surrounding and leading up to the City of Light is evidently similar to that of earth but much more beautiful and without blemish. One man discovered himself on a high hill, looking down on a breathtaking scene.

When I came more or less to myself I was standing alone in a wide and lofty place—so high and wide that I felt dazed and lightheaded and could only stand and stare.

For I seemed to be on the very crown of the world, and I could see—I, whose sight had never been very good—I could see as I had never seen before.

The sky above me was richly blue, and in it sailed islands of solid white clouds—the clouds which as a boy, I had always longed to fly up to and lie upon.

All round and below me I looked over endless distances—forests, rivers, lakes, and ranges upon ranges of hills, mountains, to what seemed the very ends of the world.

Noteworthy is the fact that no accounts were found where individuals observed prairies or deserts. Instead the landscapes observed consistently were mountains, hills—some of them small green hills and some tall hills with a rock or two—and valleys. It also has large empty fields with high golden grass that is soft, outstandingly beautiful, and very bright, and beautiful rolling green meadows with bright flowers in bloom. There are paths, trails, lanes, and roads through the great forest of trees and fields of flowers.

Animal Life. Although there is little mention of animal life inside the City of Light (which will be described in detail in the next chapter), there are numerous references to animals in the surrounding countryside. The most frequent references are to birds, particularly singing birds such as bluebirds and robins.

> Birds were numerous. All that I observed were of brilliant plumage, and they sang as though their very beings were filled to overflowing with exuberant joy.

Also mentioned were cattle, sheep, horses, lions, tigers, beavers, bears, squirrels, deer, and monkeys.

Three-year-old Benjamin Kent suffered a life-threatening tear in his trachea when he fell against a coffee table. He had been in a coma for five days when he unexpectedly came out of the coma and delightedly described his experience. He told his mother he went to heaven and saw Jesus who was a nice man. He said he and Jesus played with some big and little puppies in a great big garden. He also reported seeing lions, tigers, and bears but was not frightened because he was with Jesus.

Pets. A number of individuals also saw and held pets they had had on earth that had died. Two typical cases follow:

> I remember distinctly of looking down upon my physical body—but my joy was complete when into my arms sprang my little dog, young and full of life. He seemed to be overjoyed at finding me and we clung together, I caressing him and actually conscious of the smooth warm softness of his head and coat.

> As P. [a young boy] proceeded up the tunnel, Andy, the family's springer spaniel who died when P. was three years old (and whom P. loved very much), comes down the tunnel to meet P. Then, Abby (the family's deceased black cat who died right after Andy was run over), comes up the tunnel. . . . After Andy licks P.'s hand, P. pets Abby.

Evidently animals also have spirits and go to the otherworld when they die, and we will be able to see much beloved pets again.

Insects. Insects have been reported in a number of accounts, specifically butterflies, bees, and dragonflies. One man commented on the exquisite beauty of his surroundings:

> There were blue flowers, goldenrods with their heads yellow in color, and the flowers arranged in perfect pyramid clusters. Elsewhere in that most perfect of places, I saw Queen Anne's Lace being circled by large, graceful butterflies.

143

✫   ✫   ✫

Another person saw and heard "bees humming and gor-geously arrayed butterflies flitting from flower to flower." These particular insects added to the beauty and serenity of the spirit world's environment. There is no mention of any obnoxious insects such as cockroaches, flies, or mosquitoes.

Plant Life. Inevitably the first reaction when seeing the coun-tryside in the spirit world is awe. Everywhere people look they are deeply impressed with the lush beauty of the spirit world. In some respects it reminds them of earth, except that earth's vegetation is but a pale reflection of what they see and expe-rience there.

> I was in a beautiful landscape. The grass is greener than anything seen on earth, it has a special light or glow. The colors are beyond description, the colors here are so drab by comparison.

Joy Snell tried to describe what she experienced.

> I can only faintly suggest what it is like. I was in a vast, parklike garden. . . . There are flowers there in magnificent profusion and trees and shrubs and stretches of greensward, and walks and rivers and streams.
> Much of the foliage, and many of the blossoms resemble those of earth, but with the wondrous dif-ference . . . they glow.

The gardens there must be incredible.

I have seen the flowers of the far North and the exquisite flowers of the far South, but nothing can compare with the color of flowers that bloom in that Eternal Land.

I was not prepared for the sweetest revelation of all: the all-pervading aroma of heaven—the heady perfume! It was everywhere. I bent and smelled the flowers—yes it was there. The grasses also. The air was just the same. A perfume so exotic, so refreshing, so superior . . . !

I have seen good gardens on earth, but I never saw anything to compare with those that were there. I saw flowers of numerous kinds, and some with from fifty to a hundred different colored flowers growing upon one stalk.

The varieties of flowers were legion, but only a few were mentioned by name.

Over our heads was a pergola of vines, and crimson Virginia creeper, and wonderful tropical climbers, whose delicate orchid blossoms and gorgeous riots of colour were mingled with the drooping tassels of wisteria—purple, lemon and white—and bunches of ripening grapes.

Other flowers mentioned by name include nasturtiums, dahlias, tulips, roses, orchids, daisies, violets, Queens Anne Lace, lilac, goldenrod, forget-me-nots, hyacinths, dandelions, and cowslips.

The outstanding gardens on earth cannot compare with

the brilliance and splendor of those in the spirit world according to all accounts. One woman said that words do not exist that adequately describe the beauty of the garden she visited. "It was more beautiful than any garden I had ever seen on earth, including the Koukenhoff Garden in Holland at tulip time."

While many people told about the beautifully arranged flower gardens, others noticed very impressive vegetable gardens. Still others saw or found themselves in vast fragrant orchards with trees laden with ripe fruit, which some individuals picked and ate.

Many reported seeing vast forests of trees filled with fantastically beautiful but unfamiliar trees. Some saw majestic trees whose soft shadows gave the feeling of peace and rest. Among all the beautiful but unknown trees were a few familiar ones, specifically huge oak, hickory trees, elms, chestnuts, poplars, birches, and beeches.

Under these magnificent trees, covering the hillsides and valleys, was soft silky grass that swayed gently in the breeze and, in some cases, was up to the waist of the observer.

In this resplendent place, no weeds, thorns, or other noxious plants were seen. The trees, shrubs, and flowers were perfect; they had no dried leaves anywhere. Even trodding on the vegetation did not damage it. What is fascinating about all the grass, trees, shrubs, and flowers is that none of them ever grew to the point where they detracted from the beauty and symmetry of the scene. It was not only the beauty of individual flowers that impressed, but the way they were arranged in the gardens and how they complemented each other in color and size.

Water is present in the countryside of the spirit world in

all its forms and varieties. This included trickling brooks, streams, rivers, mirrorlike ponds, and lakes.

In the spirit world even the sky is bluer and the clouds more spectacular than in our mortal world.

Buildings. Much as they are in the rural areas of America, houses are scattered about the countryside. Small flower-lined paths lead up to individual homes and the houses seem to be small and occupied by individual family members. Some much larger buildings were reported, and the function of these buildings seems to be that of a type of reception and/or processing center and are generally located right on the boundary of the countryside and the city. New arrivals are brought there, where they are greeted and begin the transition to the spirit world.

Once they have recovered from the shock of their death and after they have been prepared, a decision has to be made as to whether they are to be permitted entry into the city or sent back. Herman Stulz was met by his guardian angel at his death. After adjusting to his new body, he and his guide headed toward what he defined as paradise.

> We approached a beautiful ornamental gate . . . but my guardian angel ushered me into a waiting room . . . and asked me to wait until he had reported my arrival and obtained permission for me to enter paradise.
>
> I entered a well-lighted room; it had windows all around, small square windows. . . . The light came from the outside, it seemed.

> While I stood there, the first thought that entered my mind was, I wonder what kind of employment I will have and what kind of work would it be?
>
> But I was greatly disappointed when I heard a strong and penetrating voice say, "Go back and finish the work that you promised you would do. . . ."

Isaac Black, upon arrival in the next world, was also greeted by an angel. This angel told him to wait while he checked the records. Upon completing his check, the angel told him that he could not enter paradise as his work on earth was not yet finished. However, he was permitted to visit his family briefly before being sent back.

Louis Tucker also found himself in a busy building.

> I emerged into a place where many people were being met by friends. It was quiet and full of light, and Father was waiting for me. He looked exactly as he had in the last few years of his life and wore the last suit of clothes he had owned. I did not think about the people or the clothes or the place, but about him, though I knew without looking that the place was not very large . . . and did not need to be, because it was only one of many entrances into the city. I knew there was a city beyond the gates in front of me. . . . I wished to go through the gates into the city but was stopped.

In these receiving stations, a number of important activities appear to take place. First and foremost, the decision is made as to the status of each individual. Once it is determined that he or she will be staying, clothing is prepared for them, relatives and friends assemble to welcome them, and guides or escorts may be assigned. The person is then prepared to enter the city.

Countryside Activities

The countryside is the place where people rest from their cares and where they can, in reality, stop and smell the roses. Besides helping prepare for life in the City of Light, people are given the chance to explore and adjust to the ethereal beauty of the spirit world. They are not pressured, even if there is someone waiting for them. For example, one woman commented:

> Time didn't seem to matter, I felt like I had all the time in the world just to stroll down the lane and enjoy the feeling of peace and serenity. I felt something was waiting for me at the end of the lane, but I felt there was no need to hurry. . . .

The term "heavenly rest" certainly seems to apply to the conditions in this place. Individuals are permitted to walk through the countryside, to enjoy the beauty of the afterworld, to engage in quiet contemplation and peaceful solitude. People are observed standing, enjoying the splendor of their environment. Some are in small groups chatting and others sitting on a rock high on a mountain and enjoying the view. Children are often seen at play, walking with their guardians or being taught. Others have been reported sitting on fences, resting under trees, or strolling through heavenly flower gardens.

The longer individuals were in the countryside and the farther they traveled, the more impressive their surroundings became, as attested to by Heber Hale.

> I moved forward, feasting my eyes upon the beauty. Everything about me was glowing in indescribable peace and happiness which abounded in everybody and through everything. The farther I went the more glorious things appeared.

In this realm they are also welcomed by family and friends and helped to adjust to their new life. William Pelley describes his sudden arrival into the spirit world.

> I became conscious that I had been borne to a beautiful marble-slab pallet and laid nude upon it by two strong-bodied, kindly faced young men . . . who were secretly amused at my confusion and chagrin [because of his nudity].
>
> Somehow I knew those two men—knew them as intimately as I knew the reflection of my own features in a mirror. And yet something about them, their virility, their physical "glow," their strong and friendly personality, sublimated, as it were, kept me from instant identification.
>
> And they knew a good joke about me. They continued to watch me, with a smile in their eyes. I got

down from my marble bench and moved about the portico till I came to the edge of a pool.

"Bathe in it," came the instruction. "You'll find you'll enjoy it."

I went down the steps into the delightful water. And here is one of the strangest incidents of the whole "adventure." When I came up from that bath I was no longer conscious that I was nude. On the other hand, neither was I conscious of having donned clothes. The bath did something to me in the way of clothing me. What I don't know.

But immediately I came up garbed. . . .

Pelley was embarrassed by his nudity, so, conscious of this, his escorts provided him privacy and clothing. Once "properly" clothed, he received visitors. Those who visited him were "conventionally garbed" (wearing clothing normally worn outside the City of Light).

Pelley's escort was very concerned about his well-being, and he was always in Pelley's vicinity keeping an eye on his whereabouts and deportment. Unlike some of those mentioned in the chapter on the spirit body, Bill Pelley knew he was dead. But he still felt as embarrassed by nudity as he had in his lifetime, and these feelings were respected by his escorts. He was given time to adjust to his "new" status and to preserve his sense of dignity and propriety.

Herr Pettersson was also received by messengers who covered his nakedness and took him to a place where he met his parents, grandparents, other relatives, and some friends who had assembled in his honor. Before he was permitted to travel, he was gradually taught many things necessary for living in this new world. Even then he was not permitted to travel alone and was accompanied by his "guardian angel." Apparently there are many things that new arrivals must learn before they are permitted to enter the City of Light.

To support the evidence that the City of Light and the beautiful countryside are not one and the same, a Native American chief who had died and come back to life reported that he traveled through paradise to the city of the dead. However, the City and the countryside are both sections of the otherworld.

Leaving the Countryside for the City of Light

Surrounding the City of Light and separating it from the countryside is some kind of a barrier that limits access to the City. Access seems to be through a control "gate." Stulz, Black, and others discovered that they were denied access to the City because they had not completed specific obligations back on earth.

However, we have accounts from individuals who were permitted to see beyond the gates and, in some cases, to enter the City of Light. One such individual said:

> Off in the distance . . . I could see a city. There were buildings—separate buildings. They were gleaming, bright. People were happy in there. There was sparkling water, fountains . . . a city of light, I guess, would be the way to say it. . . . It was wonderful. There was beautiful music. Everything was just glowing, wonderful. . . .

Summary

The countryside is a place of beauty, of peace, and of tranquillity. Its landscape is beautiful and without blemish. There is a variety of animal life, including pets. There are insects such as butterflies and bees. There is plant life with flowers and forests. The most outstanding gardens are also found there. Houses are scattered about the countryside as well as larger buildings. The countryside seems to be a place where people rest from their cares and where there is a slow lifestyle.

One thing seems to be definite: the slow and easy lifestyle of the countryside stops at the gates of the City of Light. As we shall see, the City of Light is a virtual beehive of activity. If an individual's goal is to lie back and enjoy an eternal life of quiet solitude and contemplation, the City of Light is not the place to be.

CHAPTER 10

The City of Light

In NDEs, many reports tell of being drawn toward a brilliant light, but a light that is in no way blinding. Amelia Genova was critically injured in an automobile accident and dying when she was brought by a multitude of angels toward a light that became more and more shining. She felt only peace and sweetness and complete happiness. This experience removed all fear she had of death and helped her cope with her pain when her son died nine months later.

Most individuals do not experience an NDE. But those who do, like Amelia, are permanently altered by the experience. Not only is their fear of death removed, but they become much more sensitive to the needs of their family, friends, and acquaintances.

Very few individuals have been privileged to see the City of Light. They report that the glow of the City is not the result of the reflected rays of the sun as it would be on earth but is an actual emanation of light from the City. There is no need for a sun because everything in the City produces light, a light that not only enables residents and visitors to see, but also seems to be related to the sense of peace, acceptance, and understanding that is all-pervasive.

[My guide] next led me to a city. It was a city of light. It was similar to cities on earth in that there were buildings and paths, but the buildings and paths appeared to be built of materials which we consider precious on earth. They looked like marble, and gold, and silver, and other bright materials, only they were different. The buildings and streets seemed to have a sheen and to glow. The entire scene was one of indescribable beauty. . . . There was a feeling of love and peace.

After soaring for a while, she [the angel] sat me down on a street in a fabulous city of buildings made of glittering gold and silver and beautiful trees. A beautiful light was everywhere—glowing but not bright enough to make me squint my eyes. . . .

And then I saw, infinitely far off, far too distant to be visible with any kind of sight I knew of . . . a city. A glowing, seemingly endless city, bright enough to be seen over all the unimaginable distance between. The brightness seemed to shine from the very walls and streets of this place and from the beings which I could now discern moving about within it. In fact, the city and everything in it seemed to be made of light. . . .

The beauty of the countryside was incredible but even it could not compare with the splendor of the city because of the glow.

Plant Life in the City

Betty Eadie enjoyed the gardens of the City of Light. She was allowed to go on at her own pace and to stop and study the magnificent flowers.

The garden was filled with trees and flowers and plants that somehow made their setting seem inevitable, as if they were meant to be exactly how and where they were. I walked on the grass for a time. It was crisp, cool, and brilliant green, and it felt alive under my feet. But what filled me with awe in the garden more than anything were the intense colors. We have nothing like them.

When light strikes an object here, the light reflects off that object in a certain color. Thousands of shades are possible. Light in the spirit world doesn't necessarily reflect off anything. It comes from within and appears to be a living essence. A million, billion colors are possible.

The flowers, for example, are so vivid and luminescent with color that they don't seem to be solid. Because of each plant's intense aura of light, it is difficult to define where the plant's surface starts and stops.

Nearly 140 years earlier Marietta Davis had also seen the City of Light and tried to describe its wondrous qualities. She saw a great city with majestic flowering trees and blossoming shrubs and vines. There were fountains of living waters flowing through marble channels or through beds of golden sands, while others rose to lofty heights and then flowed into glowing streams. She said the entire city appeared to be one garden of flowers and a sea of fountains with the most beautiful architecture and landscape. Immortal light encircled every object in the city.

These accounts are typical of all accounts, in which every feature of the City of Light seems to blend together harmoniously, perfectly, and beautifully, with the flowers, shrubs, and trees complementing the physical structure of the buildings.

Arrangement of the City of Light

The City is surrounded by massive walls made of brilliantly hued material (often described as jasper or other precious stones). In its walls are gates through which people must pass to gain access to the City. Streets (though not required by the residents for movement) separate the buildings and lead to various areas in the City. Some of the streets are made of material that resembles marble, while others appear to be paved with solid crystal-clear gold paving stones.

Houses. Mary Hales, who was being escorted by her brother, was permitted to look at the residential areas of the city. She reported seeing

> many beautiful homes. I was surprised to see while many of the homes were spacious, others were very small. Some were barely larger than a small kitchen or a large bathroom. I couldn't imagine why anyone would want to live in a house so small. I asked my brother about this.
>
> "That was all the material they sent up," was his strange reply.
>
> "What do you mean?" I asked.
>
> "That was all the good works they sent up," he replied, meaning that the size of a house one gets in paradise is determined [on earth] by the quantity and quality of the good deeds performed.

A number of individuals saw unfinished buildings in the spirit world, and one found out why. When she asked a messenger who would be the occupant of an uncompleted house, she was told it was for her, but it was not finished because she had not completed her life in the world.

Another man was walking down a street past magnificent trees and houses and passing many persons.

> Finally we arrived at the home of my other relatives [previously he had visited his grandparents], and they were glad to see me.
>
> As we went along I saw a place where a beautiful house was in the process of construction. Who was

building it, how it was being built, what materials were being used, I am at a loss to know; but grandfather told me it was being prepared for our family.

Buildings. When Eadie first arrived at the City of Light she was struck, not only by the brilliant beauty of it, but by how all the buildings complemented each other.

> As we entered it, I was impressed with its details and exquisite beauty. Buildings are perfect there, every line and angle and detail is created to perfectly complement the entire structure, creating a feeling of wholeness or inevitability. Every structure, every creation there is a work of art.

There are numerous buildings in the City of Light. These buildings are similar to those on earth yet different.

> I was in a land where there were flowers and trees I've never seen on earth. . . . It was a land where there were living beings who had a fantastic ability to build palaces and houses with big, heavy columns—palaces and high-rise buildings—shaped in forms people have never thought of here.

Harriet Ovard Lee saw a massive building of indescribable magnificence whose dimensions extended beyond her vision. She noted that just one of its pillars exceeded the size of major buildings on earth and that the building was of dazzling whiteness. A poor Hindu farmer, seeing such a building, described it as a temple with many gods living in it, probably a reference to the Beings of Light. A second Hindu farmer reported that he had been taken to a palace made of silver. Its furniture was made of silver with silk cushions. Carl Jung found himself in a glorious blue light standing before a temple. Heber Hale described a beautiful building with a golden dome that he thought was a temple.

Jedediah Grant, during his visit to the spirit world, saw many buildings.

> . . . the Lord gave Solomon wisdom and poured gold and silver into his hands that he might display his skills and abilities, but that temple erected by Solomon was much inferior to the most ordinary buildings he saw in the spirit world.

Others have described the magnificent interiors of the buildings in the City of Light. In addition to features previously mentioned, individuals have seen staircases, tables, desks, bookcases, pulpits, chandeliers, chairs, podiums, hallways, and patios. Robert Ashford's description of the room he found himself in is typical.

> I found myself in a large white room. It was beautiful. The floor was amber gold, and it reflected every image like a mirror. The walls were trimmed in gold. At one end of the room stood two large doors, also trimmed in gold.

Jean, who was deathly ill with hepatitis, found herself in a beautiful patio garden area.

There were a group of buildings. . . . I just knew they were libraries. They were educational buildings. I know that every single building was a different subject. All knowledge in the universe was stored in those libraries. I was excited because I wanted to go and study and read everything.

Darryl, who was a builder, was electrocuted when lightning struck his house. He found himself in a brilliant city of light looking at an awe-inspiring building which he thought was a cathedral. It was built like St. Mark's and constructed with square blocks that looked a lot like plexiglass but with centers that emanated a gold and silver light. These blocks were also translucent and he could look right through them. He knew that the cathedral was a place of learning because he could literally feel information coming at him from every direction.

Others who have reported seeing libraries include Eadie, Bob Helm, and George Ritchie. Ritchie observed that

> I lit in front of the largest library I had ever seen. It was bigger than all the buildings in downtown Washington, D. C. put together. It housed the holy books of the Universe.

Ritchie saw a pattern to the arrangement of the buildings he saw, like a well-planned university. He entered one of the buildings and

> moved down a high ceilinged corridor lined with tall doorways. The atmosphere of the place was that of a tremendous study center with wide halls

and curving stairways. Through open doorways he glimpsed enormous rooms filled with complex equipment, intricate charts and diagrams, controls, and elaborate consoles. He described visiting other buildings, like a studio where very complex music was being composed and performed, a vast library filled with documents on parchment, clay, leather, metal, and other materials, and a space observatory.

Bob Helm reported seeing a research laboratory and an art gallery.

Some of the buildings seemed to serve as places of evaluation of new arrivals and where decisions were made as to their destination. One woman was escorted by a group of men into one of the buildings. She said:

> It was beautiful inside, with mahogany, and cherry wood, and . . . [words failed her] just beautiful.
>
> We walked up a winding staircase which was crowded with people. At the top of the staircase we entered a room that was similar to a courtroom. . . . In the middle of the room was a large elongated oval table with chairs all around it. In the corner there was a fenced-off area with a beautiful engraved fence. There was a platform behind the fence in sort of a closed circle. I was asked to stand there. The men [who accompanied her] they went and sat around the table. They began to discuss whether or not I should be allowed to stay or go back.

Arthur Ford found himself standing before a dazzling white building. He entered it and was told to wait in an enormous anteroom.

> They said I was to remain here until some sort of disposition had been made of my case. Through wide doors I could glimpse two long tables with people sitting at them and talking—about me.

Larry Tooley, who was killed in a construction accident, was met by a friend who was also named Larry, with whom he had grown up and who had died six years earlier. Larry told the young man he was to be his guide until he became oriented. This young man's occupation was in construction, and he therefore took a keen interest in the composition of the construction materials and various architectural features of the rooms and buildings he observed.

> The room seemed to be made of crystallized marble of a soft pink hue. Another door, opposite the one I had entered, opened onto a street. Several low benches of white crystallized marble were against the wall. The doorways in the room had no doors, and the window openings had no panes.
>
> Larry and I left and entered the street. I was acutely aware of everything around me. I've never felt more alive. I felt like I had returned home. I knew where I was and where I was to go. We had only traveled a short distance down the street, when I stopped beside a building that I recognized. I had

frequented it on many occasions. I told Larry I had
to go inside before we could go any further.

Inside, a group of men were having a meeting. I
felt it was important that I talk with them. I spoke in
earnest, imploring them to reconsider my premature
entry into the spirit world. I knew somehow that I
had died prematurely and had not finished my work
on earth. Emphatically, I drove my point home by
pounding with my fist on the corner of a desk.

What is particularly fascinating about this account is that
this man recognized the area of the City where he was, realized that he had lived there before, and knew exactly where he
had to go to plead his case. He must have made his point, as
he was permitted to return to life.

Other buildings were evidently places of instruction.

> . . . we came into a large and beautiful city, far
> superior to any I had seen. The buildings were not
> highly ornamented. They stood in simple grandeur.
> The streets were wide and paved and perfectly
> clean. They were bordered with trees and flowers,
> whose beauty could not be told in words.
>
> In the midst of this stood a marble structure of
> four stories, covering nearly an entire block. As we
> came before it the angel said, "We will go in here."
> Immediately a door opened and a beautiful young
> lady, whose face was radiant with joy welcomed us in.
>
> I looked over the large, well-lighted, well-arranged
> auditorium. I was pleased with its beauty and sim-
> plicity. The speakers' pulpit was in the center of the

hall, fully twenty feet lower than where I stood. The seats were arranged in a circle beginning on a level with the speakers' floor, and rising, each tier higher than the other, so that the speaker could see everyone present and they did not seem to be very far away from him. I estimated an audience of ten to twelve thousand seated all in a state of expectancy.

Multiple Cities

When Lorenzo Dow Young apparently died, he was met by a heavenly messenger who was to be his guide. Lorenzo asked for permission to speak to his wife and sister before he left (they were grieving his death) but was told no. His guide said, "Now let us go."

Space seemed annihilated. Apparently we went up, and almost instantly were in another world. It was of such magnitude that I formed no conception of its size. It was filled with innumerable hosts of beings, who seemed as naturally human as those among whom I had lived. With some I had been acquainted in the world I had just left. My guide informed me that those I saw had not yet arrived at their final abiding place. All kinds of people seemed mixed up promiscuously, as they are in this world. Their surroundings and manner indicated that they were in a state of expectation, and awaiting some event of considerable moment to them. . . .

Again my guide said, "Now let us go."

In a moment we were at the gates of a beautiful city. A porter opened it and we passed in. The city was grand and beautiful beyond anything that I can describe. It was clothed in the purest light, brilliant but not glaring or unpleasant.

The people, men and women, in their employments and surroundings seemed contented and happy. I knew those I met without being told who they were.

My guide would not permit me to pause much by the way, but rather hurried me on through this place to another still higher but connected with it. It was still more beautiful and glorious than anything I had before seen. To me its extent and magnificence were incomprehensible.

This man visited three unique places, a place where people were yet to reach their assigned place, a city of light, and a second city of even greater grandeur beyond the previous city of light. He pleaded with his guide to remain and was told he was

permitted only to visit these "heavenly cities," for I had not filled my mission in yonder world; therefore I must return and take my body.

John Powell had a similar experience when, in his words,

a personage came and said, "Come!" My spirit left my body and went with my guide who took me to the next planet. Here I beheld the inhabitants. The houses and trees were beautiful to behold. I was so amazed and delighted that I requested my guide to permit me to stay and dwell there, for all things were far superior and in advance of this world that I had come from. He answered, "No," and said, "Come!"

He then took me to the next kingdom which so exceeded the first in beauty and glory that I was again amazed and requested permission to stay. I cannot command language to describe the beauty of the inhabitants and scenery, but my guide said, "No, come!"

He then took me to the next kingdom which was far more beautiful in glory and order than the former two. The beautiful flowers, trees, gardens, people who were dressed in pure white, and so pure that I was overwhelmed with joy and most earnestly implored my guide to allow me to stay, but he said, "You cannot go any further, for this is next to the throne of God." He then said, "Come!"

He then brought me again to this earth. When I saw my body lying on the bed I did not want to enter it again for I felt so happy out of it that I could not bear the thought of entering it again, but he said, "Enter," and I had to obey.

Darryl, the man who was electrocuted when his home was struck by lightning, found himself moving toward lights. As he drew closer to the lights he realized they were "cities" and that the cities were built of light.

Others have reported seeing children playing in big golden

"cities" and seeing busy people in "cities," from which it is possible to infer there is more than one city in the spirit world.

Eadie and Ritchie, as well as the Swedish scientist Emanuel Swedenborg, each observed multiple levels in the hereafter. Howard Storm had an extensive experience in which he also observed multiple levels in the otherworld.

The Native American chief White Thunder, during his visit to the world of spirits, was shown by his spirit guides "various areas of the spirit world—some containing happy spirits and others peopled by unhappy evildoers."

Herr Pettersson was also permitted to visit the spirit world and discovered, much to his surprise, that even the worst in heaven exceeded the best on earth.

> To Herr Pettersson the world of spirits resembled the material world. There were many countries, or "Kingdoms." There were cities and villages, temples and palaces, flowers and animals of great beauty and variety. The people were very busy. Some were preaching on street corners and in assembly halls, and all had great congregations.
>
> "Who are they?" Herr Pettersson asked (referring to the preachers)?
>
> "They," his guide answered, "belong to the church of the First born, and they have been sent here to be ministering spirits to those who shall yet become heirs of salvation."
>
> "I am afraid," stammered Herr Pettersson, "that I do not comprehend you. Are we not in heaven? How can the world of salvation be preached here?"

"No brother!" the guide replied, "We are not in what mortals call heaven! This is Hades."

Pettersson was ultimately permitted to visit "heaven" and its indescribable beauty. While there, he discovered that heaven also has multiple levels, and inhabitation of each level is contingent on one's diligence on earth and in heaven.

But no matter what level or city a person qualifies for, each city is so superior to any on earth that it is indescribable, and each succeeding realm is indescribably better than that immediately below it. It seems that the assignment to a specific city is contingent on the actions and attitudes of the individual while on earth. The key that opens the gate to a specific city of light is the ability to dwell in the light of that city, and this evidently depends on behaviors during earth life.

Intercity Travel

Travel seems to be relatively free from the higher realms to the lower, but not the reverse. Visits may be permitted, but only with escorts or guides. Entrance to specific buildings, areas, or even cities may be guarded. Reasons for limiting access, both stated and implied, include the protection of individuals from being exposed to environments they could not withstand; to keep people from disrupting the work of those already in the city; to protect sacred areas from people who do not or cannot appreciate them; and to keep people out of areas in which they do not need to be or are not qualified to enter.

Summary

The cities of light are just that: they are very bright and literally emanate light. No sun or extra source of light is needed or apparent. There are no areas of darkness. The cities of light appear to be filled with beautiful gardens, flowers, shrubs, and trees that perfectly complement their physical structures of walls, gates, streets, houses, and various buildings with their magnificent interiors and furniture.

There are several cities built of light on different levels, and each appears to have a greater grandeur than the last one. Those who cannot tolerate the light of a particular city are not found there. All of these cities are so superior to any on earth that it is indescribable.

There is intercity travel that seems relatively free from higher to lover realms, but restricted from lower to higher realms.

CHAPTER 11

Life in the
City of Light

Besides the indescribable beauty of the City of Light, the most remarkable feature of the place, unlike the countryside described in chapter 9, is the intense level of activity.

> I don't remember a tunnel or bright light or anything like that, only that I found myself in one of the most pleasant, busy places one can imagine.

This man was not actually in the City, but only at one of its entrances, but even from there, those he saw were extremely busy. And his brief glimpses into the City provided only a vague idea of the level of activity that goes on there.

Another man, whose death certificate had been signed and arrangements for burial made while he was dead, reported:

> It's a place of intense light, a place of intense activity, more like a bustling city than a lonely coun-

try scene, nothing like floating on clouds or harps, or anything of that sort.

Arthur Ford was also very impressed with the involvement and joy of those he saw.

Everyone there was busy. They were continually occupied with mysterious errands and seemed to be very happy.

Lorenzo Young, who was permitted to see several Cities of Light, saw busy men and women who seemed to be contented and happy. Herr Pettersson also saw busy people, as did Ford and Harriet Lee. Jedediah Grant was deeply impressed with the organization he saw in the spirit world.

I have been into the spirit world two nights in succession and, of all the dreads that ever came across me, the worst was to have to again return to my body, though I had to do it. But oh the order of righteous men and women; I beheld them organized in their several grades, and there appeared to be no obstruction to my vision. . . . I looked to see whether there was any disorder there, but there was none; neither could I see any death nor any darkness, disorder or confusion. . . . The people were organized in family capacities; and when he looked at them he saw grade after grade, and all were organized and in harmony.

Ella Jensen was taken by her guide into a very large building, where she met many people, all of whom appeared to be extremely busy, and she said that she saw "no evidence of idleness whatever."

Everyone, even small children, seem actively involved in some pursuit. For example, George Ritchie noted:

> Everyone we passed in the wide halls and on the curving staircases seemed caught up in some all-engrossing activity; not many words were exchanged among them. And yet I sensed no unfriendliness between these beings, rather an aloofness of total concentration.
>
> Whatever else these people might be, they appeared utterly and supremely self-forgetful—absorbed in some vast purpose beyond themselves.

This "vast" purpose was felt by all those observed in the City of Light and provided an overarching purpose and order. With common objectives, coordinated efforts, and effective administration, there was no overlapping of responsibilities, conflict, or disorder. Nevertheless, the level of activity and the reluctance of some individuals to leave their tasks unfinished left some observers sensing a strong degree of urgency.

Families: The Basic Social Unit

The basic unit of the City of Light, according to Grant, is the family. This is supported by the observations of James E. Johnson (the secretary of the navy at the time of his experience). He was projected into the City of Light after his car was involved in a major accident. He went rapidly through a dark tunnel toward a bright light, where he began to see people as the darkness left. There he saw the streets of a bright and totally beautiful city. The first image he recognized was his son, Ken, who was dressed in a white garment. Ken asked his father to take care of his wife and children. Then he saw his father-in-law, mother, and father. They were all together, even though his parents had never met his father-in-law on earth. James said they were together and he could feel the love among them. They also wore the same white clothes as his son, Ken.

Johnson was excited to meet his son and parents and surprised to discover that his father-in-law was there as well. He discovered that they were all a part of "his" family. As noted in earlier chapters, those most often seen by those who are near death are close relatives (parents, grandparents, siblings, children, grandchildren, cousins, aunts and uncles, spouses, and so on). Family ties seem to be extremely important, and given that they do not have other pressing obligations, relatives congregate to welcome the dying person into the spirit world as part of their family.

A four-year-old boy's NDE was the result of a two-story fall from his bedroom window. Rocky later told his mother that Jesus had taken him by the hand and they went to heaven. He told her, "There were homes there, too, only they were kind of cloud-like. People had families, and they lived in homes like here." Rocky said he did not want to leave, but that Jesus told him it was okay for him to come back, "because we are all going to be together as families in heaven." Rocky was willing to come back because Jesus said to him: "I promise you."

Mrs. Spaulding had been mourning the death of her aunt when she also died and met her aunt. This experience gave her a sense of peace and comfort and assured her that the family is forever.

> I know that mountains and valleys, rivers and lakes, trees and flowers, are more real there than here, and, best of all, our loved ones live to love and welcome us home when we are called upon to change to a higher life.

Dorothy Whippo had been terribly ill with typhoid fever when she died. She reported moving down a dark corridor toward a light in a doorway. When she entered the doorway she discovered she was in a room where her father, her brother and his wife, and her favorite uncle sat around a table. She said it was wonderful to be with them.

Martha Todd, a college professor, died from an allergic reaction to the anesthetic she received for some minor surgery.

> I came out of this tunnel into a realm of soft, brilliant love and light. The love was everywhere. It surrounded me and seemed to soak through into my very being. At some point I was shown, or saw, the events of my life. They were in a kind of vast panorama. All of this is really just indescribable. People I knew who had died were there with me in the light, a friend who had died in college, my

grandfather, and a great-aunt, among others. They were happy, beaming.

Kent Johnson was killed when a tree he was cutting flipped back and speared him in the back. His first emotion was that of terror. He did not want to die and leave his young family. In the beginning his pain was excruciating. Then,

I noticed that the pain was completely gone and I had no discomfort at all.

The earlier fear and disappointment were replaced by peace and a definite feeling of well-being. Everything was okay. Everything was just as it should be. As this feeling came, I emerged out of the darkness and became aware that I was not alone. I felt the presence of people before I actually saw anyone.

As I looked, I saw my first wife, Carol, my mother who had died in 1977 from a stroke, and my Grandfather who had died in 1974. He had been in his late eighties or early nineties when he died.

It seemed very natural that Grandfather should be there. He was always our family patriarch.

Being reunited with my loved ones, especially my first wife filled me with the greatest feelings of love, acceptance and overwhelming sweetness. . . . They had come to meet me and escort me to the spirit world—if I chose to go. They told me that I had a choice. I could stay or go. They did not try at all to persuade me one way or the other, but they expressed concern for Crystal [his wife] and the kids if I decided not to return.

176

Carol was not jealous of Crystal at all. There was not the least bit of pettiness, envy or resentment. In fact, she stated that she was . . . very concerned for Crystal's well-being if I left.

I was overjoyed to see her again and bask in her love and warmth and was not eager to be separated again. She told me not to worry about our separation, that time was not the same in the spirit world. She said life was very short, that I should return and complete my responsibilities to Crystal and the children, and then we would be together again.

Granddad had white hair but appeared to be in his early forties. Mom was in her late twenties or early thirties like I remembered her when I was very young. Carol was as I remembered her in her middle to late twenties. She had brown hair. All of them wore loose-fitting, white robes. Mom's and Carol's robes were the same basic design, though slightly different.

The young plumber Larry Tooley, who was killed when he fell from some scaffolding and who met with some men and insisted that he had died prematurely and must be allowed to return to his family on earth, then saw a large group of people waiting for him and his escort.

As we came up to them, the closest member of the group approached me—a beautiful young woman dressed in the whitest, most brilliant robe of the finest material I've ever seen. Her complexion was white and creamy, her hair jet black in color. She was overjoyed to see me and threw her arms around me, embracing me fondly.

She said she was my sister who had died when she was just three days old. Everyone else in the group was a relative who had died. They were all extremely happy that I was there. We talked, it seemed, for hours. They thought I might be granted a second chance to go back.

For those who are supposed to die, members of their families busily prepare for their arrival. In the following case, a woman saw family members getting ready for her aunt's death. The place where she found herself was so beautiful that she did not want to leave. She pleaded with her mother to let her stay, but her mother said:

> "No, you can't, it's not your time to stay." The woman continued her pleading, "Please, Mum, it's so lovely here, I don't want to go back." But her mother was very firm and would not allow her to cross the threshold. She then said to her mother, "You seem to be expecting someone; if it's not me, then who are you expecting?" Her mother said, "We are getting ready for your Auntie Ethel. She is expected shortly."

Later, when her condition had been medically stabilized, her family was permitted to visit her. While there they reluctantly told her that they had some bad news. Auntie Ethel had died unexpectedly of a sudden heart attack.

Some individuals were surprised to discover that not all

members of their families were there. Jedediah Grant, however, learned the reason for these significant voids.

> To my astonishment, when I looked at families
> there was a deficiency in some, there was a lack, for
> I saw families that would not be permitted to come
> and dwell together, because they had not honored
> their calling here. . . .

James LeSeuer was taken by his guardian angel to the City of Light and into a very large building. In the building he visited several rooms, in one of which he saw his brother teaching vast multitudes of people. His guardian angel then said:

> "We will now pass into other rooms." The next
> large hall contained thousands of people arranged
> in classes some with teachers, some studying alone,
> and they were deeply interested in the lessons and
> books they were considering. We then went into an-
> other larger hall where there were other thousands.
> These seemed to be of a much lower order of in-
> telligence. They were quarreling and jangling. There
> was a veritable hub-hub of confusion. I was in-
> formed that all in both of these rooms were rela-
> tives who were being prepared to be brought to a
> state where they could eventually be ready to hear
> and accept the Gospel. . . . Those in the last room
> lived upon the earth during the dark ages and at the
> period of great wickedness and ignorance. It would
> take ages to redeem them.

This last experience illustrates clearly that the family in the spirit world is more than the immediate siblings, parents, grandparents, cousins, aunts, and uncles of any individual. A family includes all individuals who are related to each other in any way, and this includes distant ancestors. Each individual is important to the family, and every effort possible will be and is being made to reunite the entire family.

In a few cases entire families may be needed in the City of Light to do work for their larger family. John Anderson, his wife, and his son, James, and daughter, Isabella, were brutally murdered on October 29, 1915. During his trip to the spirit world, Heber Hale was approached by John and asked to relay this information to those of his family still on earth:

> Tell the children that we are very happy, and that they should not mourn our departure, nor worry their minds over the manner by which we were taken. There is a purpose in it, and we have a work to do which requires our collective efforts and which we could not do individually! Heber was told that the work was that of their family's genealogy.

Clothing Worn

In only a few cases did individuals report being without clothing after they "died." In these cases they were quickly supplied with clothing to reduce their embarrassment and then were introduced to family and friends. How these and other people got their clothing is rarely discussed, as most people find themselves clothed and seem more impressed with what and whom they see than with what they are wearing.

During his near-death experience, DeLynn wondered:

> If I came into this world naked, how do I leave the world? I looked down and saw that I was dressed in a white garment, tailored like a jump suit. The material had a thick weave to it, yet it had the softest feel of any material I had ever felt. It was softer than silk and it glowed. The color of the material was the whitest white I had ever seen. The suit covered most of my body. Starting with a snug, but comfortable neckline, it had full sleeves to my wrists, and full legs to my ankles. A curious part of the suit was that it had no openings such as those we need as humans.

Elizabeth Marie, who experienced her NDE as the result of a teenage drug overdose, discovered that she was clothed in a white robe that covered her arms to her wrists. "The robe started at my neck and went to my ankles—it was pure white."

Clothing, apparently, is quite important, because some individuals have seen people in the City of Light preparing clothing for expected arrivals. As Hale was about to return to his physical body, he observed the following:

> As I was approaching the place where I had entered, my attention was attracted to a small group of women preparing what seemed to be wearing apparel. Observing my inquiring countenance, one of

the women said they were preparing to receive a friend of mine, Philip Worthington. He died two days after my experience in the spirit world and I spoke at his funeral.

Betty Eadie and others have seen people sewing, weaving, and being taught how to sew. Eadie, intrigued by what she was seeing,

> went closer and picked up a piece of the cloth that they were weaving. Its appearance was like a mixture of spun glass and spun sugar. As I moved the cloth back and forth, it shimmered and sparkled, almost as though it were alive. The effect was startling. The material was opaque on one side, but when I turned it over I was able to see through it. Being transparent from one side and opaque on the other—similar to a two way mirror—obviously it had a purpose, but I wasn't told what the purpose was. The workers explained that the material would be made into clothing for those coming into the spirit world from earth.

People have been seen in clothing ranging from gum boots and fishing clothing to brilliant white robes. The clothing worn appears to reflect three major factors. The first factor seems to be the position occupied by the beings in the spirit world. Those who are beings of light are always seen in white clothing, usually white, loose-fitting robes. The robes are quite similar in appearance but are still unique to the wearer, possibly reflecting personal taste.

The second factor seems to be associated with the length of time the person has been in the spirit world, his/her spiritual preparedness before they died, and the location of the individual in the spirit world.

The third factor seems to be associated with the activities of the individual. When engaged in official business, white clothing—usually white robes—seem to be required. For those doing other types of work, there seems to be a greater variety of color and style. Various individuals have reported seeing spirit beings clothed in robes of varying pastel colors such as brown, blue, beige, and green.

It also appears that clothing may be worn to help the observer identify the individual. Maureen was able to recognize her grandparents quickly because they were dressed as she last remembered them. A man was able to recognize his father because "he was dressed in his standard gray trousers and a cardigan. He hadn't changed a bit." This is probably also the reason why Ella Jensen saw her uncle Hance in his dark clothes and long rubber boots while everyone else was dressed in white. His clothing confirmed that he was dead and, in fact, had drowned while salmon fishing. A five-year-old boy, while he was drowned, saw his deceased mother wearing a black onyx cross with seven flashing stars. When he told his father about his experience and the cross, his father stiffened and abruptly left the room. His wife had died three days before her birthday and he had slipped her present (the cross with seven stars) into her folded hands, something the child couldn't possibly have known about. In this case the clothing and jewelry she wore were probably intended to verify the validity of the child's experience to the father.

The newest arrivals seem to wear the clothing they were

wearing at death—at least at first. Soldiers killed in action were seen in uniform, while period clothing and burial clothing were also observed. It seems that the stronger the individual's bonds with their earth life and the greater their addictions to earthly substances (drugs, alcohol, etc.), the less likely they were to be seen wearing anything other than earthlike or dark-colored clothing. It would appear that until they have become oriented and are prepared to live in the City of Light, clothing is more apt to resemble what they were used to wearing on earth.

Most NDErs describe otherworld clothing as being a robe and being white. The robe may be flowing and loose fitting and of a silky material and may be worn with a belt or sash, shroud, and white sandals.

Regarding the attire of angels, Ann, a forty-two-year-old lady, gave a detailed description of the clothing worn by a guardian angel.

> It seemed as if she were a pure crystal filled with light. Even her robe glowed with light as if by itself. The robe was white, long-sleeved, and full length. She had a golden belt around her waist and her feet were bare.

Social Identities

It is evident that significant friendships continue beyond the grave. As noted earlier, it is not unusual to find friends congregated with family to welcome new arrivals. And if family members are not available to welcome and help the new arrival to become oriented, friends may be given this privilege.

Eadie, for example, discovered that friendship is eternal. When she died three men in light brown robes came to help escort her. They informed her that "they, with others, had been my guardian angels during my life on earth. But I felt these three were special, that they were also my 'ministering angels.' " These three men informed her that they had been with her for eternities, and she slowly began to remember their relationship "before."

Rocky, the four-year-old boy mentioned earlier, said that he had a nice visit with Jesus. He said that the

> Heavenly Father also visited him. When asked, "How do you know the difference between Heavenly Father and Jesus?" Rocky responded, "Heavenly Father had light hair and Jesus has dark hair."

This observation of a four-year-old boy is the only one discovered where someone saw both personages and specified physical distinctions—the color of their hair.

It would seem that one's name, identity, and relationships persist beyond the grave. However, interests may be different. Things that may have seemed important on earth are supplanted by what is really important. This will be discussed further in chapter 15.

Major Activities

Family. In general, most activities seem to revolve around the family in one way or another. People gather to meet new family arrivals from the earth. They also meet to decide whether the new arrival should remain or return, and some become involved in a lively debate as to the individual's capabilities and the probability that he or she will actually complete work the family needs doing, as was the situation encountered by the following individual.

> . . . in the distance, was a throne-type, high-backed chair, with a personage in it. I couldn't distinguish a face, but I felt that this personage had some higher power in the spiritual realm. The people seemed to be the judge and the jury for my situation.
>
> At the left side of me stood my grandfather, Rey L. Pratt, whom I never knew in this life, and my grandmother, Mary Stark Pratt, his wife, who had passed away three months previously. . . . Through thought transference I knew that I was on trial for my life. The trial was to determine whether or not I would be allowed to continue in this life—based upon whether I would do the things I was supposed to do, and cease transgressing.
>
> My grandfather felt that I probably would not be able to continue. Evidently there was some mission I was supposed to perform. He felt that they might have to select someone else, because I wouldn't be able to carry it out. I apparently was not a strong

enough character to follow through with whatever I was supposed to do.

My grandmother took my defense and said that she thought that I would, and she said I should be given the chance to prove that I could do this. I of course, didn't understand fully what they were talking about, except that I wanted to go on living.

So it was decided—my grandfather looked at me, and at this other person in the chair, and they kind of viewed each other—and it was unanimously decided among them, through thought transference, that I would be given this chance.

Other activities engaged in the spirit world include teaching the newly arrived what they need to know to progress into the City of Light, helping them become adjusted to their new life, introducing them to other family members, encouraging them to fulfill responsibilities to their earthly families and to fulfill their commitments to the rest of their family in the spirit world. These family responsibilities will be covered in greater detail in chapter 15.

Work. Perhaps the greatest problem facing those who have died is that of adjusting to and finding their "niche" in the City of Light. Louis Tucker met his father, and they both wanted to get caught up on the news, his father about what was happening back on earth and he of what his father had been doing.

I wanted to know how he was, if he had a home in the city, if he had yet settled to any definite work there, and many other things. I gathered that not only his clothes but his appearance were different when he worked, that he did have a home, which we would share, that he had glorious friends, that he had definite employment. . . .

The word "work" does not reflect the same meaning it has on earth. Work here is often forced on us, may provide few rewards, and may be demeaning and/or alienating. This is not at all the case in the spirit world or City of Light. For example, Bob Helm died during surgery and found himself with a being in a white robe.

. . . we arrived at another location, on a beautiful street. We appeared to be alone there, except for the street-sweeper, who was responsible for the spotless condition of the place. Here again, the colors and textures were outside my experience; and the road and the sidewalks appeared to be paved in some kind of precious metal. The buildings appeared to be constructed of a translucent material. I felt prompted to talk to the street-sweeper and congratulated him on his efforts. He said work was a joy to him, and he derived his pleasure from doing the best job he could at all times. This statement nonplussed me somewhat, for I had never been enthusiastic about what I considered menial tasks. This man appeared absolutely sincere, however; and I was very impressed by his industry and the obvious love and care he brought to his work.

Apparently there is no "menial" work in the spirit world or City of Light. All tasks contribute in some meaningful way to the development and welfare of the inhabitants of the City of Light, or to the beautification of the City, or to the desires of the Being of Light, and are therefore automatically worthwhile. As noted earlier, there is no idleness, confusion, or conflict in the City of Light. Order, love, and service seem to dominate the attitude and objectives of everyone who dwells there.

A number of those who had extended visits to the spirit world and City of Light discovered that individuals take the skills and abilities they developed on earth with them into the spirit world, where they are used to help accomplish heavenly objectives.

Specific activities and work observed by those who visited the spirit world and City of Light include learning and gaining knowledge; service as ministering spirits to those of a higher level; teaching; performing in musical organizations such as choruses, orchestras, bands, and choirs; gathering genealogical data; checking records and reporting new arrivals; watching over mortals as guardian angels; preparing clothing for anticipated spirit world entrants; missionary work; guiding newcomers; serving as messengers to earth and other areas of the spirit world; constructing buildings; cooking and other kitchen duties; caring for animals; gardening and maintaining the landscape; planting and harvesting; research; keeping records; guarding gates and entrances to buildings; and conducting meetings.

Administrative Councils

Contact between those who live in the City of Light and those in other areas of the spirit world and on earth seems to be restricted. As mentioned earlier, observers saw no confusion or disorganization in the City of Light, and permission had to be obtained to contact persons not in the same city. Individuals who live in the City of Light must petition or be assigned some earthly responsibility to be able to visit the earth.

Both Henry Zollinger and Lerona Wilson were told by those in the spirit world not to mourn their deaths, as they had important tasks to accomplish, and that the intense grief of their loved ones on earth was impairing their ability to do their work.

Those who feel that their deaths were premature and that they should return to earth also have a formal procedure to follow. They must appear before a panel of individuals in order to plead their case or have their cases pleaded for them by family members. Success or failure of a petition seemed to be contingent on the person's willingness and ability to complete some work. Some were sent back because they had not yet completed the work they had promised friends and relatives they would do even before they were born. Still others were sent back in response to fervent prayers of the living or to do work for those in the spirit world that they could not do for themselves. Individuals may not have been told what work they still had to complete before they would be permitted to stay, only that it was important to those on both sides.

Various individuals told their living relatives that they had to get permission to return even for only a few moments. For example, one NDEr, after petitioning the authorities, was given permission to come back and tell her relatives not to weep for her, and she asked them not to call her back. She told them to be glad, for the spirit world is far more wonderful than anything they could image.

Activities in the spirit world are tightly controlled. People are not allowed to wander around exploring on their own. They are escorted at all times and guards are placed strategically about the city to assure that important functions and activities are not disrupted or to protect individuals from going places for which they are not prepared. Possibly the guards are not protecting secrets as much as they are providing security for sacred functions and areas.

Summary

It seems quite clear that everyone in the spirit world and especially in the City of Light has something meaningful to do, knows how his or her work fits into the greater scheme of things, and is willing and happy to perform any assigned duties. There is no such thing as menial or degrading work there, nor are individuals forced to do anything they do not want to do. People are taught but not forced to accept what they hear. If people wish to do something outside of their assigned responsibilities, they have to request permission to do so. Petitions are seriously considered, and the petitioner probably knows the decision ahead of time. All petitions are heard by a council of elders or a panel of judges. In the case of requests to return to the physical body, a primary consideration is the individual's prior performance, the probability that the individual will complete the work he or she is supposed to, and the needs of the larger family unit. Decisions are based on the collective impact that they will have on the immediate family unit on earth and on the larger extended family in the spirit world. All decisions have eternal implications for both the individual and his or her family.

CHAPTER 12

The Purposes of Post-Earth Life

Love seems to be the guiding principle of post-earth life, and its overall purpose is the perfection of everything. At least, this is what Jack Ausman was told by an angel, who said the one great power that animated all those in the heavenly dimension was "divine love." He further stated:

> We have only one object set before us—the betterment of all life and all things. We follow this, our mission, with humility and simple trust in Divine Love.

Various NDE accounts suggest there are four main purposes of post-earth life. These purposes are teaching others, gaining knowledge, gathering and keeping records (particularly family records), and serving others.

Teaching

The primary function of the otherworld seems to be instructional in nature and probably the most important work in this world is the teaching of eternal truths. The evidence from some NDEs indicates that a tremendous process of education takes place in post-earth life. As noted earlier, people are organized by their various abilities and are instructed according to their understanding and actions while still on earth.

Individuals are seen leading multitudes of people, standing before vast congregations, and teaching children of all ages. One woman who was in the otherworld for some time while undergoing an operation indicated that beings started to instruct her in various spiritual matters.

Henry Zollinger, who saw his deceased older brother in the otherworld, found him teaching a large congregation. When he finished, the brother told Henry that he was very happy in his labors. John Peterson is another NDEr who saw individuals teaching a great number of people.

Peter E. Johnson was given his choice whether to return to life or remain in the spirit world. When he asked what he would be doing if he remained, he was told that he would be asked to teach the spirits there.

Some individuals were informed that close relatives were needed to help teach there. This was the case with Merrill Nerville, who told his sister while she was in the spirit world "that so many of his grandpa's people had been killed in the war that his grandfather needed Merrill to help him with his work among his kindred dead." So there was a definite reason why this person died, and evidently it was important for his

family to understand that he was all right, happy, and working hard.

Gaining Knowledge

Closely related to the teaching of others is the process of
gaining knowledge.

John Oxenham had an extensive visit to the spirit world
after he died and learned about the importance of education
in the otherworld as well as about the activity of helping others. His son Hugo served as his guide and escort.

> ... now tell me, if you can, some things that
> have always puzzled me. All the people I have seen
> here seem intensely absorbed and happy.
>
> "Of course," said Hugo, "Because, here, we are
> all round pegs in round holes. There are no misfits.
> We are all doing the work for which we are best fit-
> ted, and that makes us all happy."
>
> "How do we find our jobs?" I asked him.
>
> "Well," he said slowly and thoughtfully, "there
> are two things we've got to do here—continue our
> own education for the higher spheres—and help
> those who are needing help, either here—or else-
> where—or still on earth. And we naturally want to
> help in the ways we know best."

While Zollinger was in the otherworld he observed that
people have their free agency just as we do here and that gaining knowledge was the only way to progress.

Marshall Gibson talked of people in the City of Light busily working on spiritual matters and learning new things.

Raymond Moody wrote that NDErs described an entire realm of the afterlife set aside for the passionate pursuit of knowledge. He and Ring found that NDErs come away from their experiences emphasizing the importance of seeking knowledge on earth and that it continues in the otherworld.

George Ritchie also saw a realm of knowledge and stated, "It is this realm which removes forever the concept that we stop learning or progressing in knowledge when we die."

So possession of knowledge appears to be required for progression and development in the otherworld. However, while every attempt is made to help new arrivals learn that which is necessary to progress in the spirit world, no one is forced to accept what is being taught, although they are forced to be quiet and respectful.

Record Keeping

There is evidence from the number of requests made by relatives in the otherworld to NDErs to return to life so they can gather information on family members to suggest that record keeping is an important activity and a purpose of life in the otherworld. For example, Johnson was informed

> that my progenitors had made a request that if I chose, I might be granted the privilege of returning, to again take up my mortal body, in order that I might gather my father's genealogy. . . .

196

Harriet Beal, who traveled to the otherworld, saw a large room filled with individuals rapidly documenting family records.

Serving Others

George Gallup was one near-death researcher who compiled evidence from NDEs indicating that service to others was a major purpose of life in the otherworld. He surveyed those who had visited the spirit world about what they saw the citizens of heaven doing. Their responses tended to fall into one of three categories:

1. They minister to the needs of others in heaven.
2. They minister to the needs of others on earth.
3. In addition to interpersonal ministries, they have certain jobs or duties assigned to them within the heavenly hierarchy.

Serving others in the otherworld is illustrated by a comment made by Jedediah Grant's deceased wife. When he asked her the whereabouts of three other personages, she replied, "They have gone away ahead, to perform and transact business for us."

Gallup mentions the example of a young woman who said she thinks all needs are met in the afterlife because they are anticipated before they occur.

Those in the otherworld also serve those who are still alive on the earth. One NDEr said inhabitants of the otherworld continually pray for those on the earth. A major service to mortals from those in the otherworld is watching over them as guardian angels. In this regard, two NDErs saw or spoke with their guardian angels, one of whom specifically mentioned that he followed the NDEr constantly while he was on the earth. NDErs have also been promised that they would receive the constant support and guidance of a guardian angel.

Summary

The four main purposes of post-earth life seem to be teaching others, gaining knowledge, gathering and keeping records (particularly family records), and serving others. These purposes of the post-earth life give a general feel for what things are of most importance there. Clearly NDE research gives evidence that life, work, and activity continue in the otherworld, just as it gives evidence that people go to the otherworld after earthly death.

CHAPTER 13

Angels

In the many accounts of lengthy NDEs there are very few instances where the individual did not meet an angel or angels. In some cases the angel announced that he or she was the person's guardian angel. Usually, however, the individual assumed that the being he or she saw and/or conversed with had to be an angel. This chapter examines the experiences reported by those who had deathbed visions or NDEs to see what can be learned about these angels—who they are, their abilities, appearance, and the role they play. There will be some overlap between the materials covered here and what has been covered in earlier chapters because of the fact that the designation "angel" has been assigned to any being that emanates light, wears clothing that dazzles the eye, or possesses qualities thought of as being angelic. Various individuals who have met or seen beings with extraordinary qualities assume, often from their religious conditioning, that these beings have to be angels. Some individuals recognized or discovered that their angelic visitor or escort was a close relative or friend who had preceded them into the spirit world. For most, however, their angelic host was someone unknown to them. Whether there are angelic beings who permanently inhabit the City of Light and are assigned to watch over specific inhabitants on earth or whether the "angels" are former residents of earth who have achieved angelic status is not clear. In this chapter the focus will be on what people reported they saw and not on what they thought or speculated it meant.

Appearance and Abilities

The primary quality that defined personages from the after-life as "angels" for most people was the light that enveloped them and emanated from them. For example, a man being rushed to a hospital when his heart stopped reported being surrounded by a black cloud and going through a tunnel and coming out at the other end in a white light. There stood his brother, and behind him was an angel of light who encompassed him with love.

A second person was stopped by a "brilliantly lighted person" who knew his thoughts and reviewed his life.

Ritchie reported seeing two beings that exuded brilliant light. He also felt intense love flowing from them.

A ten-year-old boy experienced a cardiac arrest.

> I was met at the end of the tunnel by a bunch of people. They were all glowing from the inside like lanterns. The whole place was glowing in the same way, like everything in it was filled with light. I didn't

know any of the people I met there, but they all seemed to love me very much.

Kathy, a mother of two children, reported that she was sent back to life by a being of light. But it was more than just light, it was light that feels and understands. In her case, the Being of Light touched her and filled her whole body with light.

Four-year-old Ann had the following beautiful experience with an angel.

I noticed a light coming into my room. It was a beautiful golden-white light which seemed to appear in the wall to the left of my bed.

I sat up and watched the light grow. It grew rapidly in both size and brightness. In fact the light got so bright that it seemed to me that the whole world was being lit up by it. I could see someone inside the light. There was this beautiful woman, and she was part of the light: in fact she glowed.

Her body was lit from the inside. It seemed as if she were a pure crystal filled with light. Even her robe glowed with a light as if by itself.

She called me by name and held out her hand to me. She told me to come with her. Her voice was very soft and gentle . . . but it was more in my mind.

I asked her who she was and she said she was my guardian and had been sent to take me to a place where I could rest in peace. The love emanating from her washed over me so that I did not hesitate to put my hand in hers.

A nine-year-old boy reported that when he died he passed through a dark tunnel and was met on the other side by a group of angels. When asked if they had wings, he said they didn't, but

> They were glowing and all of them loved him very much. He was told by a being of light that he had to go back and reenter his body.

Little Daisy Dryden also reported seeing angels and that they did not have wings. When asked how they get around, she replied. "They don't fly, they just come."

A man also saw angels without wings. In his words, "I saw angels, they were floating around like you see seagulls."

Judith Reeves reported that when she died, "Two white angels came to me. They lifted my spirit from my body and glided away with me to a city of light."

During her NDE, a young woman found herself out of her body looking down at it lying unconscious on her bed.

> I was joined by a radiant being bathed in a shimmering white glow. Like myself, this being flew but had no wings. I felt a reverent awe when I turned to him. This was no ordinary angel, but had been sent to deliver me. Such love and gentleness emanated from this being that I felt that I was in the presence of the Messiah.
>
> Whoever he was, his presence deepened my serenity and awakened a feeling of joy as I recognized my companion. Gently he took my hand and we flew through the window.

Encounters with angelic beings of light have also been reported by Native Americans. For example, Chief White
Thunder reported that he "saw two spirits dressed in snow
white robes, who asked me to go with them."

In summary, angels have distinct identities. Those who see
them not only see beings, but beings that emanate light. Their
bodies and their clothing glow with a light that can be both
seen and felt. These beings have hands that can be touched,
faces that radiate love and acceptance, bodies that suggest
strength and power, and a definite sexual identity. In short,
they look much like people on earth but with qualities that set
them apart. For example, one of Michael B. Sabom's patients
reported:

> I was floating in air toward a wide open door with
> light all around Jesus, who was in the door. Behind
> him was a long staircase with angels lined up the
> stairs. . . . It was pure light, light gold, and so beauti-
> ful. There were also people, all kinds of people.

Though this individual did not specify the differences he
saw between "people" and "angels," they must have been significant if he could distinguish between them.

During her visit to the City of Light, a woman discovered
that she was not alone. Behind her was a tall, masculine-looking
figure in a robe. She sensed they could go wherever they willed
themselves to go and be there instantly. She said they communicated through projection of thought and they seemed to
be on some universal wavelength.

Two characteristics many people have been conditioned to
expect of angels are wings and halos, neither of which has

been reported. In fact, many individuals specifically mentioned that the angels they met or observed did not have wings.

From the preceding accounts, it would appear that angels are not limited by time, space, or physical barriers, yet they do have substance. Various individuals not only saw angels, but felt their touch. They saw them as solid, not translucent beings. Yet these angelic beings were able to pass through walls, closed doors, and windows. The angels did not need any physical means, such as wings, to travel between the earth and the spirit world, and they "knew" when and where they were needed. They were able to communicate with humans through thought in whatever language the person spoke. There were no problems in miscommunication, as the intent of the angels was completely understood by every person.

Angels not only can communicate effectively with all individuals, they also understand what the individual is thinking. Questions were answered before they were asked, concerns addressed, and fears eliminated. The angels also had an aura about them that could literally be felt. Individuals knew that they were safe and loved, not because the angels told them, but because they felt it. Love, peace, and acceptance radiated from the angels and was experienced as a total emotion.

Angels clearly have a quality about them that no mortal has.

Roles of Angels

The implied or stated purpose of angels' visits sometimes was to inform or warn but usually was to assist the individual in some important way.

Protectors. Most individuals' experiences with angels was in their role as guardians. Their primary purpose seemed to be to watch over them, heal their wounds and afflictions, and protect them from their enemies. Don Fearheiley has collected twelve accounts in support of this perception. In his book *Angels among Us,* he relates "amazing true stories of ordinary people being helped by extraordinary beings." Included in his book are accounts where angels stopped a car from hitting a five-year-old girl, saved a teenage girl from drowning, cured a young man's malignant tumor, guided a young child lost in a forest to safety, helped a hunter who had accidentally shot himself reach help, warned a driver to stop his car (thus avoiding a serious accident), and saved a man from death when the ladder on which he was standing fell. Hope Mac-Donald, in her book *When Angels Appear,* has assembled a similar collection of accounts of angelic interventions. Among some of her more interesting accounts were where angels healed a young woman of a malignant tumor; ordered a physician not to start his car so as to prevent him from backing over a two-year-old boy who was playing unseen behind it; brought a woman who had been raped, then shot three times, to a place where she could get medical help; saved two young children from being hit by a speeding car; ordered a navigator on a World War II bomber to move to the rear of the plane, which saved his life when a shell penetrated his ship just where he had been sitting; saved several very young children who had been playing with matches from being burned to death; and protected a shopkeeper from being robbed and beaten.

One of Fearheiley's accounts involved a fireman who was responding to a major warehouse fire. He raced to his car, jumped in, and turned the ignition key. Then he twice heard a voice say to stop and get out of the car and look behind it. When the fireman finally got out of the car, he found his little niece Marie playing with her back against the back bumper of the car. He believes the voice was that of her guardian angel.

Beth Armstrong was sleeping with her baby, Beverly, when she heard a voice calling out to move. She thought she was dreaming and continued sleeping until the same voice said a little louder to move. As she turned over and was about to go back to sleep, she heard the voice a third time say loudly, "Move, Beverly." A few seconds after she moved the child who was sleeping with her next to the wall on the other side of the bed, a heavy picture fell from the wall landing exactly where the child had been lying. She believes that the voice was that of an angel sent to save her infant's life.

In September 1982 Rachel Clark was driving her Volkswagen van to pick up her daughters when she was told by a voice as clear as if someone were sitting beside her to get out of the car. This command was repeated several times until she finally pulled over to the side of the road and stopped. She quickly got her three-month-old daughter and fourteen-month-old son as well as her three-year-old daughter from the car. They ran about ten feet from the van when it exploded into flames. It happened so fast that she felt without the warning it would have been impossible for her to react fast enough to save any of her babies, and possibly not even herself.

Twelve-year-old Mark Durrance was out walking his dog, Bo, when he was bitten by a large rattlesnake. Mark told of a man who picked him up and carried him to the house. He said the man had a deep voice, blue eyes, and strong arms and wore a white robe. The man told him he was going to be really sick, but he would be all right. This young child not only saw his guardian angel, but felt his arms about him, saw what he was wearing, and received assurance from him that he would be okay.

Children have reported having their lives preserved by angels. Two small children had fallen into a canal. Their lives were saved, so both reported, by a "beautiful person, all white and shining, who stood beside them in the water, held them up, and guided them to shore." A third little girl heard the scream of their nurse and ran up just in time to see a "lovely lady in the water dragging the two children to the bank."

One case tells of a small infant being protected from being burned to death by someone all gloriously white and silvery. Another child was protected from being trampled to death by a team of horses. The child told her mother, "Oh, Mama, I am not hurt, for something all in white kept the horses from treading upon me and told me not to be afraid." Two very young children became lost in a forest. The children told their parents that they had gone to sleep under a tree and were awakened by a beautiful lady with a lamp, who took them by the hand and led them home.

The wife of a nationally known talk host was protected from a rapist by an angelic being. When her car broke down on a freeway she pulled off the road to wait for the police.

Soon a car pulled in front of her car, and she waved through the window for the driver of the car to go on. But he kept coming back and she thought that he didn't see her, so she rolled down her window to tell him that she was waiting for the police. When she did that, he got into her car. Suddenly, as the man was attempting to rape her, a man emanating a bright light appeared right between the rapist and her. The rapist ran for his car and left, and immediately the light and the man disappeared.

In these accounts it was assumed that the extraordinary individuals helping were guardian angels.

Constant Companions. In 1898, a young man was stricken with malaria and had an NDE.

> My spirit left my body, just how I cannot tell. But I perceived myself standing some four or five feet in the air, and I saw my body lying on the bed. . . . something attracted my attention, and upon turning around I beheld a personage, who said: "You did not know I was here?"
>
> I replied, "No, but I see you are. Who are you?"
>
> "I am your guardian angel. I have been following you constantly while on earth."
>
> "What will you do now?" I asked.
>
> He replied, "I am to report your presence, and you will remain here until I return."

From this, it could be assumed that at least some individuals have angels that have been assigned to watch over them as constant companions. This young man discovered this after

208

he "died," and the discovery had a significant impact on his subsequent life and actions.

In another account, a woman learned as a child that she had a constant companion and one in whom she could confide any time. During her NDE as a child she met a guardian angel named Sarah. Although the experience occurred twenty years earlier, Sarah was a constant companion who always appeared to provide solace and advice on earthly problems. The woman always thought Sarah was invisible to other people until her teenage son came home late one night when the woman and her guardian angel were having a heart-to-heart talk on the problems of raising a teenage boy. He peeked around the corner and saw them. The next day he asked his mother who the woman was and said that she seemed really nice.

Consultants. In at least one case a guardian angel was sent to consult with a young soldier preparing for battle during World War I. On October 22, 1918, Charles A. Shirley

> discovered someone sitting by my side. Where he came from or how he joined me without my hearing him I did not know. I did not ask him his name. Without any explanation on the part of either of us, we began to talk. He spoke to me saying, "Three days you will fight in a battle at Verdun, and you will fall critically wounded. If you were given your choice, on what part of your body would you choose to be wounded?"
>
> I thought a moment and then answered, "If I were shot in my legs, no doubt I would lose them

and be crippled for life. If I were shot in my right arm, perhaps I would lose my arm."

I paused a moment and continued, "If I am to be given my choice, let me be shot in the left side, in the shoulder, the arm, or the hand."

Without comment the stranger replied, "You have your choice."

Three days later we were making another attack. I had carried a message a mile back to headquarters and was standing watching the charge while waiting for my return orders. As I waited, a shell burst near me. Another passed over me. Then I heard another shell coming. Something seemed to tell me that it would get me. I was wounded in the left side, shoulder, arm, and hand, just as I had chosen to be.

Guides/Escorts. Regardless of the actions of the angels, most people see them as guardians. As will be shown, the term "guardian" is a broad umbrella that includes such activities as guide, escort, guard, messenger, and even warrior.

Many individuals who were permitted to look into the spirit world shortly before they died saw angels waiting for them. Twelve-year-old Minnie Chatham, shortly before she died in 1873,

> sat up in bed and said, "The angels have come for me. I must go! They are at the door waiting for me."

John Peterson reported becoming aware that an extraordinary being was with him in his room.

It was between ten and eleven o'clock that a visitor suddenly made his appearance in the room and, standing by the couch on which I lay, placing his hand in my hand asked if I was ready to go. I answered, "yes" and just at that instant I seemed to stand upon the floor, my body lying on the bed. . . . we started off on our journey through space, seemingly with the rapidity of lightning. I asked my guide who he was. He answered he was one of the guardian angels sent to bring the dead.

Due to complications associated with her pregnancy, a young woman's spirit left her body. She saw a bright light and someone coming toward her. He was an angel who had come to get her. She didn't know who he was, but he was someone who had always helped her.

Harriet Ovard Lee heard a voice calling her name, saying

"Harriet," three times, "Come, I am waiting." I did not recognize the voice. It seemed as if I awakened up out of my sleep. . . . The voice said, "Come," and I saw a personage whom I followed downstairs, and we passed out at the door into what appeared to be unlimited space. Again my guide called me by name, commanding me to follow him, which I did.

An Indian chief, White Thunder, saw two "spirits" who asked him to go with them.

In 1921 Herman Stulz saw a strange man who was clothed in a robe standing at the foot of his bed. He greeted Herman with a smile and invited him to come along with him. Herman was concerned about how he would find the spirit world, but his guide only said, "Follow me" which he did.

Upon arrival, Herman was ushered by his guide into a waiting room and told to wait until he had reported his arrival and gained permission for Herman to enter.

Blanch Henderson, of Windham, Ontario, Canada, was joyously visiting with her deceased friends and relatives when her guide told her to bid farewell, for she must return to the physical world. Herr Pettersson had an extensive visit to the spirit world, some of which was reported earlier. He was permitted to travel in the spirit world accompanied by his guardian angel, who also served as a guide.

Groups of Angels

Mike, a nine-year-old boy who was killed when he fell off a 250-foot cliff, heard beautiful music.

It was a multitude singing something like hymns, or humming. The sound was unbelievable. . . . There were angels, thousands of angels, dressed in white robes. They were kneeling down with their arms outstretched, and they were singing.

A woman was sitting with her dying child. His four-year-old brother was in a separate bed in the same room. The little brother woke up and, pointing to the ceiling, with every expression of joy said, "Mother, look at the beautiful ladies round my brother! How lovely they are; they want to take him." His brother died at that moment.

Amelia Genova died while having her leg operated on. As she died, she was lifted up by a multitude of angels and taken toward a light.

A young boy reported seeing many angels as he died.

> Mother, here is Grandmother, come! You must see her! And she is with a great company, and they are come to take me away with them.

Lily, a child of three, also saw a number of angels accompanying her aunt, who was waiting for her.

> . . . she looked up to the ceiling saying that she saw her aunt calling her, surrounded by little angels. "Mother, how pretty."
>
> From day to day her illness increased, but she always repeated, "My aunt has come to fetch me; she is holding out her arms to me," and as her mother wept, she said, "Don't cry, Mother, it is very beautiful, there are angels round me."

Activities of Angels in the City of Light

Herman Stulz observed that there was perfect order in the spirit world, with rules and laws no spirit could ignore. When they arrived, his guide had to report his arrival and gain permission for him to enter. Some angels were seen writing records of significant events on earth. Others were checking records to see if the new arrival was ready, worthy, and qualified to enter specific areas in the City of Light. Some reported to other angels the arrival of individuals to the city. Angels were seen guarding gates to keep the unqualified from entering particular areas. Some angels were observed teaching and orienting new arrivals, and others were providing comfort and support not only for new arrivals, but for those still on earth. A number of angels were seen convened to hear petitions and requests either to remain in the City of Light or to be permitted to return to earth.

Angels were sent to inform individuals that they could not stay and that they had to return to their earthly bodies. Kim, a fifteen-year-old girl, "blacked out" during an operation on her leg. When she came to:

> I was standing there, and I saw this brilliant light—not like heat-warmth—more peace-warmth. I got curious, and started going toward it. I heard someone call my name. I turned to look, and there was this lady.
>
> She was dressed all in white. Her hair was white, and it was flowing down her back—it came to about her knees. She was really pretty. She was glowing, not just from the light in the distance, but

from herself. She called me by name and said: "It's not your time." I didn't quite understand, and she repeated the message; that it wasn't my time, and that I had to go back.

Angels have been seen and heard singing in choirs. The sound of angelic choirs has been described as unbelievably beautiful and in perfect harmony.

I knew these beautiful beings to be angelic. They sang the most lovely and extraordinary music I had ever heard. They were identical, each equally beautiful. When their song was over, one of their number came forward to greet me. She was exquisite. . . .

Identity of Some Angelic Beings

Some angels turn out to be someone the NDEr had known while on earth. It often took some time for them to realize that they knew the angel due, in part, to their extraordinary appearance. Individuals reported to have discovered their angelic escort was their grandmother, brother, close friend, or wife.

There is a fascinating account of an eight-year-old boy who died shortly after his deathbed vision.

"Oh, what a wonderful sight! See those little angels."

"What are they doing?" asked his sister.

"Oh they have hold of hands, and wreaths on their heads, and they are dancing in a circle around me. Oh, how happy they look, and they are whispering to each other. One of them says I have been a good little boy and they would like to have me come with them." He lay still awhile and then seeming delighted exclaimed, "See there come some older angels—two at one end and two at the other."

"Do you know any of them?"

"Yes, Uncle E. (who died about six months before) but there is a whole row of older ones now standing behind the little ones."

"Do they say anything to you?"

"Yes, but I can't tell you as they tell me, for they sing it beautifully. We can't sing so."

"Can't you tell what they say?"

"Keep still, don't talk, and I will listen and tell you. They say, 'Come little J. and be happy with us.' Grandma is speaking now. She says I'm a good little boy and if I come now, she will take care of me. Uncle E. is speaking now and says, 'Write and tell them I am happy.' He says if I do not get better I shall come and be with him, in a world of love and joy. Oh, this is Sally [his mother's sister who died in her youth before his mother's marriage]. She says I have a good mother, but if I don't stay with my mother, I shall go and be happy with Aunt Sally, and she will be like a sister to me.

In this account, the child not only saw little angels, but some of the angels turned out to be close relatives—an uncle, his grandmother, and his aunt Sally.

The discovery that some angels they encountered were close relatives surprised some individuals but delighted all. To realize their departed loved ones were watching over them as guardian angels and would be there to help them in their transition from this life to the next was very comforting.

Warrior Angels

While some angels have been classified as protectors, others judging from their appearance, clothing worn, and their possession of weapons could be identified as warriors. For example, James Beck reported seeing

> an angel standing just above my head where I lay— defending the house. Standing upright with a drawn sword in his right hand extended above his head and his face lifted up to heaven facing due east. He was tall and stood very erect. He was clothed in a complete suit of armor with a helmet cap or covering upon his head. It appeared and shone like pure silver. I saw plainly the joints at the knees and arms.

Beck's account was from the 1860s, while the following was reported 130 years later.

In 1993 two young female missionaries, responding to a request to know more about their church, visited the home of a man. Not much was said by him the entire time they were there. They did not feel at ease and left quickly when their presentation was complete. Feeling relieved, but not knowing why, they hurried home.

Several days later the man was arrested for murdering a number of young women. In investigating his activities, the police discovered that the two young women had been alone with him in his house. The police asked the man why he had not killed them when he had the chance. He replied, "I had planned to kill them, but when they sat down, I saw behind them two of the largest, most powerful men I have ever seen. They were armed with weapons I have never seen before. I knew without any doubt that if I tried to hurt them, I would instantly be destroyed."

In the next two accounts, entire armies of warrior angels were seen. The first was recounted by Luiz Carlos. Luiz had visited the interior of Brazil as a Christian missionary. He was successful in converting many people in a small village. Their conversion to Christianity changed them profoundly, and they gave up a long history of idol making and worship. This angered the people in the next village, and they vowed to attack and kill all of them. However, the village was never attacked. They later learned from the chief of the warring village that they had started across the pass to attack the village but were confronted by a large army with drawn swords on white horses, blocking the way. They became frightened and turned around and fled back to their own village.

The second is the well-documented angels of Mons, who appeared on a battlefield in World War I. The Allies were in the middle of a terrible defeat, with many casualties. The wounded soldiers who were being taken to a hospital were telling the nurses that they had seen angels on the battlefield. After the war the Germans, when asked about the battle, said that their horses suddenly turned and fled. They said the Allied position they were attacking was held by thousands of troops. The fact was the Allies had only two regiments.

There is a fascinating account of a young woman, Diane, who had gone to visit friends and had stayed longer than she planned. By the time she headed home it was late. She was not afraid because it was a small town and she lived only a few blocks away. However, she noticed a man standing at the end of an alley on her way home. She became uneasy and said a prayer for protection. After the prayer she felt secure and had a sense that someone was walking with her. She walked right past the man at the end of the alley without incident.

The next day she read in the newspaper that a girl had been raped in the same alley after she had been there. Later she identified the man in a police lineup. She then asked a policeman if he would ask the man why he had not attacked her. When the man was asked he answered that he did not attack her because she had two tall men walking with her.

The mere presence and appearance of warrior angels prevents the evil activities of those whom they were sent to stop.

If the warrior angels could prevent wars and disasters and protect the innocent, then why do horrible events like the Holocaust occur? Howard Storm was given the reason during his NDE.

The number of holocausts that happen in the world were only a tiny fraction of holocausts that were planned by men. They, the angels, only allowed a few to happen, while men stayed awake nights trying to make them happen. They don't want any more to happen, but one of the ways they thought people could learn, to illuminate the tragedy of the holocaust, would be to allow a few of them.

In terms of a big nuclear holocaust, there isn't going to be one. They have too much invested in us and in this world. They love all the little plants, trees, animals, and people, and they aren't going to allow it to be wiped out by some idiots.

Many people throughout the world suffer fates worse than pets would be allowed to suffer. Those kinds of problems, therefore, are the really important issues. The spirit world has made it abundantly clear that those issues are what they want us to address. The spirit world is not into elitism. As a matter of fact, they despise elitism, where one person is presumed to be more spiritually attuned than someone else. They are into non-interference. They want us to do the work. It would be pointless, since they can do it effortlessly, for them to do it for us. They have, therefore, kind of a hands-off attitude about this world.

Summary

Angels seem to be those beings who carry on the day-to-day operations of the City of Light and serve as messengers from the spirit world to those still on earth. They serve as escorts/guides for those who have died, and they serve as guardians for individuals on earth. When emergency situations warrant it, warrior angels have been known to protect those who need protection.

Angels have the physical appearance of humans, with the one major exception that they glow. They are beings of light—not reflected light, but light that comes from within. This light is felt as pure love, complete peace, and total acceptance.

Whenever malevolent beings are met, they are usually in the dark, the period when individuals are moving toward the light, and seem intent on stopping them from reaching the light.

CHAPTER 14

The Realm of Bewildered Spirits

The otherworld is divided into two major realms. One of these realms has been designated in this book as the area associated with the City of Light. The other, less frequently mentioned realm is the Realm of Bewildered Spirits.

What do we know about the Realm of Bewildered Spirits? There are several accounts of evil spirits and "frightening" NDEs in the near-death literature. Maurice Rawlings, Margot Grey, George Gallup Jr. and Bruce Greyson and Nancy Evans Bush have documented most of these cases. These frightening NDEs may be characterized by one or more of the following: feelings of extreme fear or panic; emotional and mental anguish that may extend to states of utmost desperation; being lost and helpless; intense feelings of loneliness during the experience, coupled with a great sense of desolation; and a dark, gloomy or barren, and hostile environment.

Sometimes people having frightening NDEs report finding themselves on the brink of a pit or at the edge of an abyss and need all their inner resources to save themselves from plunging over the edge. Some people felt that they were being tricked into death and had to use all their inner resources to prevent it.

The heart specialist Maurice Rawlings, who has collected reports of hellish or frightening NDEs, believes that there are as many frightening NDEs as there are euphoric ones although that has been disputed by Michael Sabom. He also believes the euphoric NDEs get reported and the frightening ones do not because people are afraid to tell others about them or they tend to forget them quickly because they are too horrible to remember.

There is still limited information on the number of frightening NDEs versus the euphoric ones, but George Gallup Jr. found in his national study that a significant number of NDEs are described in neutral or frightening terms. The near-death researcher Arvin S. Gibson found in his study of the Salt Lake City region that 12 percent of the NDEs involved fear. Angie Fenimore, who had a frightening NDE, was told in the otherworld that most people who are dying today are going to a place of darkness.

Over the past few years a growing number of NDErs have been coming forward with their frightening NDEs, and an increasing number of researchers are writing about them. Three principal varieties of frightening NDEs have been identified initially by Bruce Greyson and Nancy Evans Bush and were later labeled by Kenneth Ring as "inverted" NDEs, "hellish" NDEs, and "meaningless void" NDEs. Still later another category, the "instructional" frightening NDE, was identified by Gibson.

Visits to the Realm of Bewildered Spirits

Some NDErs have had frightening NDEs where they have actually entered the Realm of Bewildered Spirits and returned to life to tell about it. To better understand the frightening NDE, a sampling of cases is presented here. These cases also give evidence of a realm of bewildered spirits.

Angie Fenimore found herself in the Realm of Bewildered Spirits when she tried to commit suicide. She was in thick blackness and saw young people dressed in black who stared blankly forward and showed no concern or curiosity about where they were. As she went farther into the darkness she saw crowds of thousands upon thousands of other people who emanated darkness and were too caught up in their own misery to have any mental or emotional exchange. She described this place as an empty world where a person could not make connections with others and the solitude was terrifying.

Karen, who was going through a divorce, also attempted suicide. She described her NDE this way:

> One night as I was lying in bed, asleep, I was awakened by a male voice saying: "I'm going to get you. Sooner or later, I'm going to get you." The event frightened me and I sat up, wide awake. I told my roommate, and she said it was just a dream, and not to worry about it.
>
> About a week later, everything seemed so hopeless that I took the bottle of tranquilizers. My full intention was to kill me. It seemed the best way to handle my problems, just to go to sleep. . . . At the hospital, I found out later, they pumped my stom-

ach and put charcoal in it. They didn't think I was going to make it. My heart had stopped, and they used defibrillator paddles to restart it.

During this period I became aware that I was conscious, but I was enveloped in total darkness. It was pitch-black all around, yet there was a feeling of movement. My conscious self assured me that I was in the form of a spiritual body.

A male voice spoke to me, a different voice than the one I heard a week before. This voice said: "You have a choice. You can stay here, or you can go back. If you stay here, your punishment will be just as it is, right now. You will not have a body, you will not be able to see, touch, or have other sensations. You will only have this darkness and your thoughts, for eternity."

Terrified because of the experience, and because of what I had heard, I understood that this would be my private hell. There would be no contact with other life or with the sensations of life, for eternity. Yet I would remain conscious with my thoughts in total blackness.

Frantically scared, I knew immediately that I had made a terrible mistake. Telling the voice that I had made a mistake, I asked to go back, to return to life. The voice said, "All right, you may return."

In another case a person experienced the following:

It was black and there was a terrible wailing noise. There were a lot of other beings there, all wailing and full of desperation. I don't know what it was. I don't even like to think about it now because I can feel the terror again. But as far as I am concerned, I was in hell.

A person suffering from TB, who one day tried to end his life by throwing himself out of a window, had this to say:

> I felt an inner struggle going on between myself and some evil force. At the last moment I suddenly felt an inner explosion and seemed to be enveloped in a blue flame which felt cold. At this point I found myself floating about six inches above my body. The next thing I remember is being sucked down a vast black vortex like a whirlpool and I found myself in a place that I can only describe as being like Dante's Inferno. I saw a lot of other people who seemed gray and dreary and there was a musty smell of decay. There was an overwhelming feeling of loneliness about the place.

Another NDEr who experienced a frightening NDE while dead for an hour following an accident stated:

> I remember more clearly than any other thing that has ever happened to me in my lifetime, every detail of every moment, what I saw and what happened during that hour I was gone from the world. I was standing some distance from this burning, turbulent, rolling mass of blue fire . . . I saw other people I had known that had died. . . . We recog-

226

nized each other, even though we did not speak. Their expressions were those of bewilderment and confusion. The scene was so awesome that words simply fail. There is no way to escape, no way out. You don't even try to look for one. This is the prison out of which no one can escape except by Divine Intervention.

Probably the most complete descriptions of evil spirits in another world is given in the well-known NDE of Professor Howard Storm from Northern Kentucky University. Storm became ill while on a trip to France and had an NDE in a Paris hospital. After leaving his body and looking at it lying in the bed, Storm was led away by some voices whom he initially thought belonged to doctors and nurses. A portion of his experience follows:

> As I asked them questions they would give evasive answers. They kept giving me a sense of urgency, that I should step through the [hospital room] doorway. With some reluctance I stepped into the hallway. And in the hallway—I was in a fog, or a haze. It was a light colored haze. It wasn't a heavy haze, I could see my hand, for example, but the people who were calling me were 15 or 20 feet ahead; I couldn't see them clearly. They were more like silhouettes, or shapes, and as I moved towards them they would back off into the haze. . . .
> I walked for what seemed to be a considerable distance, with these beings all around me. They

were leading me through the haze. I don't know how long—

As we traveled, the fog got thicker and darker. And the people began to change. At first they seemed rather playful and happy. As we traveled, though, some of them began to get aggressive. Then, others would seem to caution the aggressive ones. I seemed to hear them warn the aggressive ones to be careful or I would be frightened away.

I continued to ask questions, and they repeatedly urged me to hurry and to stop asking questions. I felt very uneasy, especially since they continued to get more aggressive. I would have returned, except I didn't know how to get back. I didn't know where I was. There were no features that I could relate to. There was just the fog and a wet, clammy ground. I had no sense of direction.

I finally told them that I wouldn't go any farther. At that time they changed completely. They became much more aggressive and insisted that I was going with them. They began to push and shove me, and I responded by hitting back at them.

It seemed to be, almost, a game for them, with me as the center-piece of their amusement. My pain became their pleasure. They seemed to want to make me hurt—by clawing at me and hitting me. Whenever I would get one off me, there were five more on me. By then it was almost complete darkness, and I had the sense that instead of there being 20 or 30, there were an innumerable host of them.

Each one seemed set on coming in for the sport they got from hurting me.

I fought well and hard for a long time, but ultimately I was spent. I lay there amongst them, they began to calm down since I was no longer the amusement that I had been. . . .

Not only did Don Brubaker see the world of bewildered spirits, he went there and was confronted by Satan. Don had rushed to the hospital with symptoms of a pending heart attack. As his doctors wheeled him into an elevator, his heart stopped, and he found himself falling feet first in what he described as a dark, damp, musty tunnel. Even though he was on his back, he could see ahead into the depths of the horrible tunnel. He saw a large glowing red ball.

Almost like the light on the front of a train. In that instant, as the red ball rushed toward me, I knew terror like never before. As it approached, I realized that it was really a large, eerie red eye. It stopped when it got close to me, and then began traveling alongside me through the tunnel. I could hardly stand to look at it, its gaze was so piercing. It felt like it was looking right into my mind, into my very soul . . .

As the red eye glowered at me, the thoughts began to arrange themselves, coalescing slowly. Suddenly, the idea was undeniable.

I was in Hell.

The realization swept over me like an ocean wave, unstoppable though I tried desperately to dismiss it. Hell! I didn't even *believe* in hell! And here I was? This was it?

I had only the briefest moment to react to the thought when a deep, comfortable voice echoed through the tunnel.

"Have no fear, my son," the voice said with a certain resounding nobility, "for I am with you. I have chosen you to write about the experience you will go through."

When Don wondered why he had been chosen to have this experience, the voice responded,

"You'll first experience hell, . . . to prove to you the reality of evil. You've only believed that there was goodness. You must see for yourself that hell is real. And then you can tell others about the awful reality of hell, and about the beautiful glory of heaven."

When Don asked, "But why me, God?" he was told,

"Because you represent common man. You're not a noted minister or a highly educated theologian. People will more easily relate to and accept your story."

After this experience with God, he regained consciousness and tried to tell his physicians and nurses. But they virtually ignored him, believing he had suffered oxygen deprivation.

He then found himself once more plunging back down the

dark tunnel and into Hell. He sensed the presence of a powerful being. This being informed Don that he could avoid all the pain and anguish if he would just follow him. Not only would all the pain disappear, he could have anything his heart desired. Then his eyes were opened. He saw,

> Visions of wealth appeared before my eyes, like a three-dimensional movie. Diamonds, money, cars, gold, beautiful women, everything. I was overwhelmed by the vision. I could almost touch it, it seemed so real.

Don realized that the tempter was Satan, who was bargaining for his soul. He struggled mightily to shake himself free of these images. He said that he could clearly hear the words, "Enjoy, enjoy" in one ear and in the other, "Resist, resist." He felt as if he was caught in a huge tug of war and was literally being torn apart. And one party to the battle was Satan, a being he had never believed existed. But now he knew with complete certainty that Satan did exist and was fighting for his soul.

Don then experienced a life review, but a hellish life review:

> ... I heard a laugh, a sniggering laugh from somewhere in the darkness. ... Images appeared before my eyes, as if projected on a giant screen.
>
> I was seeing myself. All of those times in my life when I had done something wrong were being shown back to me. As I watched, I was embarrassed, then ashamed. When the long chronicle was over, I began to watch scenes of the things I had

only wished for—worse things than what I had actually done! I watched myself participating in sin after sin—a repulsive but exciting but disgusting but exhilarating experience. My emotions became tangled and knotted.

After the review Don was feeling abandoned and lonely. He longed for his family and to be able to tell them how much he loved them, how much God loved them. Then out of nowhere he heard the voice of God. The voice told him that his mission was to tell others that there is a God and that they must learn to love others, to have compassion, and to forgive. Don was told that he must live his life so that others could see the influence and reality of God through him. God also informed Don:

> Your physical healing will take a long time, but you will live. Remember that. You will recall all of your experiences clearly, and you will write a book. You must tell others about me and about Satan. You must make them understand that there are very real choices they must make. I have chosen you for this work. You will succeed. You will be safe. I am always nearby. You are never alone.

Don saw bedraggled beings shuffling along in the "dark, damp, musty cave" blindly following each other, convinced that they were trapped in their sins and could not be saved. Don knew that if they would just look up to God, they could be saved from eternal enslavement, but they resisted. They had been so blinded by Satan that they could not believe that God would or could forgive them.

Don was not the only individual to report having seen those trapped in Hell. George Ritchie, Betty Eadie, Margot Grey, Elane Durham, Harriet Lee, and Lorenzo Dow Young are but a few who were permitted to look into this nightmarish realm, to see the condition of those dwelling there, and discover that they are prisoners of their own doubts and feelings of worthlessness. Blinded by Satanic philosophies, they could not, they would not, accept the fact that they could escape, that there was a God who could save them.

Don's message to the world is, Heaven is real and so is God. But Hell is also real and so is Satan. God is always waiting for you to turn to him. He will help you escape the clutches of Satan. Love is the essence of Heaven and everything else leads us away from love and God.

Frightening NDEs seem to have some elements in common with euphoric NDEs, while others differ. Scott Rogo has summarized a comparison of the core elements of frightening or hellish NDEs with euphoric NDEs as follows:

Phase 1: The subject feels fear and feelings of panic instead of peace and joyfulness.

Phase 2: Just as with the more classic NDE, the subject experiences leaving the body.

Phase 3: Again, similar to the classic NDE, the dying person enters into a dark region or void.

Phase 4: Instead of experiencing the presence of comforting religious figures, friendly deceased relatives, or a great white light, the subject is overwhelmed by a sense of foreboding and senses the presence of an evil force.

Phase 5: The subject finally enters a hellish environment, different from the beautiful and peaceful Elysium of the classic NDE.

Margot Grey says that those who have frightening experiences return from their NDEs with the conviction that life continues after death just as those who have euphoric NDEs do. They also feel a strong urge to modify their former way of life radically.

Gibson found that his suicide NDErs came back knowing that they should not have done it and saying they would live a better life. He also found that individuals who had frightening NDEs could point to circumstances in their lives that led to the frightening NDE.

George Gallup reported that the frightening NDEs in his study had some of the following features: featureless, sometimes forbidding faces; beings who are often present but are not at all comforting; a sense of discomfort—especially emotional or mental unrest; feelings of confusion about the experience; a sense of being tricked or duped into ultimate destruction; and fear about what the finality of death may involve.

Views of the Realm of Bewildered Spirits

Besides those who have experienced these frightening NDEs where they entered the Realm of Bewildered Spirits are

NDErs experiencing euphoric NDEs who have had the opportunity to glimpse this division of the otherworld.

Elane Durham had a view of spirits trapped in a less than heavenly realm, which she described this way:

> When I got close to the light, something on the side of my vision distracted me. I looked down and to the side and saw a host of people. Rays from the light were shining over the tops of the heads of the people, but they didn't seem to notice. They appeared to be shuffling around, and I could feel anger and confusion coming from them. It was as if they were all lost, and they were agonizing over the pain that they felt. They seemed to be earthbound and unable to see the light that was over them.
>
> As I looked at the people I thought to myself: You can go to the same place, all you have to do is, look at the light.

Harriet Lee saw a region of the otherworld inhabited by millions of miserable and unhappy occupants. She said, "They were in great confusion, wringing their hands, holding them up, and tossing their bodies to and fro in fearful anguish." My guide said, "These are the spirits in prison; they know the punishment that awaits them and they are in great distress by reason of their knowledge." Then she was shown happy inhabitants in another region. She said, "Some were reading books, some walked about, and all were busy. The children played and romped around, while the grown people, especially the men, were very busy, and it seemed to be such a beautiful place." She said to her guide, "Who are these?" "These are the spirits in paradise," he answered.

Lorenzo Dow Young was also shown the condition of those who are in this realm. His guide, after showing him the heavenly realm, said:

> "I will now show you the condition of the damned." Pointing with his head, he said, "Look!"
>
> I looked down a distance which appeared incomprehensible to me. I gazed on a vast region filled with multitudes of beings. I could see everything with the most minute distinctness. The multitude of people I saw were miserable in the extreme. "These," said my guide, "are they who have rejected the means of salvation, that were placed within their reach, and have brought upon themselves the condemnation you behold."
>
> The expression of the countenances of these sufferers was clear and distinct. They indicated extreme remorse, sorrow, and dejection. They appeared conscious that none but themselves were to blame for their forlorn condition.
>
> This scene affected me much, and I could not refrain from weeping.

Jedediah Grant saw the righteous gathered together in the spirit world with no wicked spirits among them. He also viewed the people confined to a location separate from that of the righteous.

Lerona Wilson went to an area where a large congregation of people seemed to be shut up within walls.

The Native American chief White Thunder, during his visit to the world of spirits, was shown by his spirit guides "Various areas of the spirit world—some containing happy spirits and others peopled by unhappy evildoers."

Still other NDErs have also had glimpses into the part of the otherworld where spirits are not happy. Several people have reported to Raymond Moody that they glimpsed other beings who seemed to be trapped in an apparently most unfortunate state of existence. The NDEr George Ritchie saw such a place, as did one of Melvin Morse's child NDErs.

These NDE accounts give evidence that there is an area in the otherworld with people or spirits who apparently did not follow the body of laws that govern humanity, or at least who fall into the undefined category of "wicked." The background of some of these NDErs would suggest that the meaning of the word "wicked" would have a Christian connotation.

Can a person who finds himself or herself in this realm following earth life ever escape it? People who reported seeing this realm to Moody said it appeared that those spirits would be "there only until they solved whatever problem or difficulty was keeping them in that perplexed state." Ritchie who saw a similar realm believed that once those people realized the cause of their state, expressed sincere remorse, and let go of their earthly desires, they would be given the opportunity to continue their spiritual and mental growth. This suggests the possibility of progression from one realm to the other as well as between levels.

Summary

There are two sources of information on a second realm—the Realm of Bewildered Spirits—in the otherworld. The first source is accounts of frightening NDEs, and the other is glimpses of this realm during euphoric NDEs. Those who have frightening NDEs find themselves in a dark and gloomy or barren and hostile environment. Those who have euphoric NDEs see an area of the otherworld where millions of miserable, unhappy, and wicked people are confined until, it seems, they solve whatever problem or difficulty is keeping them there.

Whatever the source of information, the Realm of Bewildered Spirits in the otherworld seems to be filled with hate, despair, terror, hopelessness, darkness, and animal passions.

CHAPTER 15

The Connection between Pre-Earth Life, Earth Life, and Post-Earth Life

Pre-Earth Life

Most people probably assume that conception is the beginning of their existence, but many NDEs suggest otherwise. During their NDEs a number of people "remembered" a time before they were born, usually in connection with commitments they were reminded that they had made for doing specific things when they came to earth. Some recognized their guides and escorts as individuals they had known before they came to earth. In one fascinating case discussed in the chapter on the location of the spirit world, a young man recognized where he was—even remembered the buildings and streets—and knew exactly where he had to go in order to plead that he be permitted to return to his family still on earth.

Betty Eadie reported being taken to a place where many spirits were being prepared for life on earth. She was told that everyone on earth had desired to come to earth. Another thing she was told was that abortion is an act that hurts the unborn child not only physically, but spiritually as well. The spirit knows that a particular body is intended to be his or hers and feels an immediate and devastating rejection when its body is aborted. Eadie also learned that experiencing life is crucial but that the length of life is not.

> I saw many spirits who would only come to the earth for a very short time, living only hours, or days after their birth. They were as excited as the others, knowing that they had a purpose to fulfill. I understood that their deaths had been appointed before their births—as were all of ours. These spirits did not need the development that would result from longer lives in mortality, and their deaths would provide challenges that would help their parents grow.

During her NDE Eadie met individuals whom she recognized as being close friends before she came to earth. Eadie also reported seeing a male spirit who wanted to be born to a specific couple and was trying desperately to get them together so that this would be possible.

Besides realizing that they had known some of the spirits they met before they came to earth, some NDErs report meeting and conversing with spirits who were expecting to go to earth in the immediate future. Nine-year-old Katie tells of playing with two young boys who were waiting for their turn to be born.

The book *Life Before Life* is a compilation of accounts of parents, primarily mothers, who saw and spoke with children who would one day be born to them. Though a majority of these cases are not NDEs, they do offer intriguing insights into the interconnectedness of earth life and the pre-earth life. From these accounts it appears that individuals have some say as to which family they will belong to on earth.

There are incidents related in this book where parents were informed by prospective children that they were waiting anxiously for their turn to join the family. One example was Karrie, who was engaged to be married in July. In May she had the following experience:

> During the night, about 1:00 A.M., I was awakened by a voice. It was a girl, standing by my bed. She was tall and lovely. I immediately knew she would be my first child. She said she loved me, and her love was heavenly. She expressed tremendous joy at the prospect of being able to come to Earth. It seemed that we already had a deep loving relationship—I had just forgotten. This experience lasted only a few moments.
>
> Nycole was born a year and a half later. She is my love and the joy of my life.

Another person who had a similar experience was Janet. Janet was fearful of pregnancy because her other pregnancies had been very difficult. She decided to have another child anyway after having the following experience:

> I was alone in the kitchen, cleaning the stove. The three older boys were outside playing, and Porter [her youngest son] was asleep on the couch. The house was quiet and peaceful. I was feeling

content with my life, when suddenly I heard "Mommy, Mommy!" I turned around, still knowing that everyone else was outside. To my great astonishment, six feet from me I beheld a little girl about five years old! I could see her perfectly clear, yet I was also aware that she was a spirit and not of flesh and blood. She was wearing a white ruffly pinafore and dress with shoulder-length hair. I knew immediately that this little girl was to be our daughter.

I did not move toward her, we just stood looking into each other's eyes. Although I had heard her with my ears when she first called me, we did not speak vocally again but communicated spirit to spirit. I knew what she was thinking, and she would answer my thoughts.

She was most anxious to come to earth—and so excited about letting me know this. She loved the boys and knew Michael and I well from our pre-earth life. I also learned that we had all chosen to be together on Earth and that she was anxious to join us. She told me that she knew I was trying to create an atmosphere that would invite God's spirit into our home, and that pleased her, because she was also a little apprehensive about leaving her Heavenly Father's presence. I learned that she had been permitted to visit me so that I would know that she was anxiously waiting.

Janet's account reveals five important details about the relationship that exists between earth life and pre-earth life. The first is that spirits can elect to join together and become families on earth. Second, they are aware of what is happening in their prospective families on earth. Third, certain types of family atmospheres are preferable to others. Fourth, spirits may be apprehensive about coming to earth. Finally, permission must be obtained for spirits to visit and communicate with prospective parents.

It would appear that to alleviate some of the fears that spirits may have before their birth, loving relatives or close friends of the family into which the spirit is to be born help. Take the case of Lee, a very close friend of Roy Caldwell, Lee who had just been killed in Vietnam. Roy was preoccupied with thoughts of the death of his best friend when the following occurred:

> I saw Lee and . . . a little girl with green-blue eyes and beautiful, radiant blond hair. She had curls all around her face and was absolutely the most stunning child I had ever seen. She ran into Lee's outstretched arms. He picked her up, placed her on his knee and began telling her about me, my wife and our home. Then with a sudden burst of excitement I realized he was talking to my little girl. He laughed and joked with her and she giggled and accepted his teasing. I awoke with tears streaming down my cheeks and realized I had seen the spirit of our unborn baby and Lee had given her final instructions before she was born.

Some people saw spirit children who appeared to be sad and were informed that their sadness was due to the plans of their prospective parents to stop having children or not to have any children. As a result these spirits would be denied the chance to be born into the family of their choice. For example, Carol already had ten children and was under pressure by her family not to have any more. One night during her evening prayers she

> beheld a beautiful garden and a marble-like bench. On the bench was seated a fully-grown personage with the saddest countenance I had ever seen. Not a word was spoken, but the message was clear, and it burned within my heart. This spirit was saddened because I was considering ending my childbearing. He wanted to be part of our family, and it was his time to come to this mortal state.

In another case, a young woman was greatly upset that she was pregnant. She had only recently married and did not feel she was emotionally or financially ready to start a family.

> I had a dream that changed my whole perspective on life. I dreamed that I was in heaven dressed all in white. I was talking with a distant voice when I saw a beautiful, young girl. She wore a white dress with an enormous white bow in her long, dark hair, and she had the most beautiful brown eyes. I spoke to the voice and said, "Who is that little girl?"
>
> The voice replied, "She is a spirit child waiting for her turn on earth."

I then asked, "Well, if she is going to earth, she should be happy. Why does this little girl look so sad?"

The distant voice answered, "She is upset because she sees how sad you are that she is coming."

I woke up the next morning knowing that I had hurt my unborn child. From that day forward, I begged the Lord for forgiveness and told him to tell my daughter I wanted her, and was waiting for her.

Some parents were informed by a child that they wanted to be born to their family, but if their preferred family was unwilling to have them, then they would be born to other parents, as it was their time to come to earth. Jerry and Dorothy had adopted a newborn baby boy, whom they had named Todd. When he was three, Dorothy's sister had an experience in which her deceased father appeared to her. He told her:

> Todd is a great spirit and was my good friend in the spirit world. When he found out his birth parents didn't want to keep him, I asked him if he would like to come to our family. Todd agreed.

It would seem to be that even though spirits are anxiously awaiting their turn on earth, they are extremely concerned about the experience. They are aware of the problems of earth life and that many spirits have failed to live the type of life that would permit their return to that place in the spirit world where the beings of light dwell. This concern is revealed clearly in the following account. In this account, Laura found herself in the pre-earthly existence, walking along with the daughter she was to bear in six months.

> I found myself walking along with my daughter. She and I were both grown women and the best of friends. She was talking to me about her worries of coming to earth and living so that she could come back here. We both knew I was to be her mother and that is why she was talking to me about her concerns. She stopped and looked at me and said, "Help me get back to Father."

These parents became acutely aware that they had eternal relationships with their children and that they assumed great responsibilities for the spiritual well-being of these children when they became parents. They also realized that they knew their children, not only as infants to whom they would be-come parents, but as individuals they had previously known, loved, and committed themselves to help. These accounts seem to indicate that the location of the pre-earth life and the post-earth life is the same, although no hint is given as to where that place is.

In some reports, parents saw their prospective children waiting with deceased relatives for their turn to come to earth.

> Lois P. related, "I was in the midst of a difficult delivery. All seemed dark and the tears coursed down my cheeks. I had endured natural childbirth six times before, but given the choice of death to re-lease me from delivery at that moment, I may have chosen it. My husband, John, leaned over me and

whispered, 'Courage, for your little one will come very soon.'

"Then at the most bleak moment, I saw my deceased mother, holding a small boy by the hand. Just as suddenly she was gone. Our baby boy, Ben, was born half an hour later."

Ann, concerned about the well-being of her daughter, who was expecting her second child, had the experience of seeing her husband, who had died sixteen years earlier.

He was smiling happily and standing beside a lovely, dark-haired girl. I knew this was our soon-to-be granddaughter, and I felt assured that all would be well.

From these accounts and many others, it appears that it is crucial for spirits to be able to come to earth as mortal beings. Evidently these spirits have some choice as to the family they will be born to. If their first preference does not work out, they will be born to other parents. They are disappointed, but evidently they are unwilling to postpone this important event once it is scheduled, and the prospect excites but causes deep concern.

Some children, such as Johnny and Jonathan cited in chapter 3, seem to retain memories of their pre-earth life in their early childhood. As time passes, these memories begin to fade, as illustrated in the following account.

A young boy asked his parents if he could spend some time alone with his new baby sister. The parents agreed, but without their son's knowledge, they set up an intercom unit next to the crib so they could monitor and record the session. From that recording, here's what the little boy said to his baby sister: "You have to tell me about God. I'm starting to forget."

Phyllis Atwater's research reveals some fascinating information drawn from children's NDEs about the intimate connection between pre-earth life, earth life, and post-earth life. She has noticed that adult experiencers will occasionally be met in death by children they will eventually father or mother, and children, even infants, are invariably greeted during their death experience by any siblings who died before them. These siblings tell the child NDEr how they died. Future children sometimes appear as well, and they give the names they would someday have. Atwater has not come across any incident where a child NDEr was incorrect about any of these past or future siblings, even in cases where it was absolutely impossible for the child to have such knowledge.

Children are active participants in the transition to and from earth. They are helping others get ready for their sojourn on earth and welcoming siblings just arriving from earth. As with adults, they also ask new arrivals about the conditions in their families yet on earth.

Earth Life

Before a person is born, not only are there specific things the individual agrees to do while on earth, but the length of time the person is to live on earth appears to be predetermined. At least in some cases, it seems a person is to live long enough to accomplish the work assigned. In other cases, however, the person is to live out a predetermined period of time. A woman's heart stopped because of an allergic reaction to an anesthetic. She said:

> I found myself in a beautiful landscape. The grass is greener than anything seen on earth, it has a special light or glow. The colors are beyond description. The light is brighter than anything possible to imagine. In this place I saw people that I knew had died. There were no words spoken, but it was as if I knew what they were thinking and at the same time I knew that they knew what I was thinking. I felt a peace that passed all understanding. I felt as if I wanted to stay there for ever, but someone, I felt it was my guardian angel, said, "You have to go back as you have not finished your term."

A young woman was informed by an angelic being that, ". . . she was too young to die and it was not time for her to go. He said I had much to live for. I was to tell the people of the world that there is life after death and that there are higher beings and a God so they could be comforted by this information."

Theresa learned that she chose those life experiences that would help her grow the most.

> "I had lived before I came into existence on this plane. The best analogy I can think of to explain it

involves a record with different grooves in it. This life is analogous to one of the grooves."

"Did you see yourself in a pre-mortal state?" [Interviewer]

"I sure did."

"What were you doing?" [Interviewer]

"I was attending to other people. There were children that I was caring for, and others. I realized that I was on a high level of responsibility; I was of service to others."

"Did you see yourself making choices?" [Interviewer]

"Yes, in fact, I chose this whole life."

"What do you mean, you chose this whole life?" [Interviewer]

"I chose the family and the difficulties that I would have during my lifetime."

"How could you have consciously chosen to live through some of the things that later befell you?" [Interviewer]

Theresa laughed and said: "That's true. Now it seems incredible that I chose to be a baby that was nearly aborted and later was adopted. At the time, though, it seemed most appropriate for my own growth. When I made those choices there was no fear because I knew I was going to come back soon. There was another important factor in making the choices—I wanted to experience all facets of emotional life.

"In retrospect, my premortal choices did, in fact, expose me to the full range of human emotions. I was aware, when I made the choices, that this would allow me to progress to a higher level. In the spirit world, I saw that we did not experience many of the sensations of earth life, such as taste, touch and smell. I wanted to experience everything possible."

A young woman's NDE was induced by severe complications associated with her pregnancy. This is what she reported about that experience.

I was filled with supreme joy. There were things I had forgotten about entirely that I was able to enjoy again in the fullest sense. I felt the sweetest joy in realizing that trials really do stack up like stairs. . . . Each trial prepares you for the next one, bringing you a blessing of knowledge or wisdom or experience. Sudden, inspiring recognition of how carefully our own individual tests are planned burst over me, and I was filled with gratitude.

Harriet Lee was told by her spirit guide:

. . . you have got to return back to the earth to complete the course marked out for you, for you have got a great deal of work yet to do. You will be tried and tempted in every way. Your troubles and trials will be great and your life will hang on a hair's breadth, but you will come off conqueror in the end. Now go, and see to it that you humble yourself and keep faithful and staunch [emphasizing the

word "staunch"] to the end. You have a mighty
work to do both for the living and for the dead.

These accounts suggest we agree to accomplish certain
work during our earth life and choose the life experiences we
will have while on the earth. The realization that we played an
active role in choosing of the problems we experience would
seem to reassure us that there is a purpose in everything even
if we do not understand exactly what it is.

Post-Earth Life

What do we take with us into the spirit world? If they do
nothing else, NDEs reveal that there is continuity in a person's identity after death. One's personality continues relatively unaltered from earth life into the spirit world. There is
no sudden transformation in what one values, desires, or has
become habituated to. For example, George Ritchie observed
the actions in the spirit world of those who had become addicted to alcohol and tobacco while on earth.

> I saw a group of assembly-line workers gathered
> around a coffee canteen. One of the women asked
> another for a cigarette, begged her in fact, as though
> she wanted it more than anything in the world. But
> the other one, chatting with her friends, ignored
> her. She took a pack of cigarettes from her cover-
> alls and without ever offering it to the woman who
> reached for it so eagerly, took one out and lit it up.
> Fast as a striking snake the woman who had been

refused snatched at the lighted cigarette in the other woman's mouth. Again she grabbed at it. And again. . . .

With a chill of recognition I saw that she was unable to grip it.

The being of light drew me inside a dingy bar and grill near what looked like a large naval base. A crowd of people, many of them sailors, lined the bar three deep, while others jammed wooden booths along the wall. Though a few were drinking beer, most of them seemed to be belting whiskies as fast as the two perspiring bartenders could pour them.

Then I noticed a striking thing. A number of the men standing at the bar seemed unable to lift their drinks to their lips. Over and over I watched them clutch at their shot glasses, hands passing through the solid tumblers, through the heavy wooden countertop, through the very arms and bodies of the drinkers around them.

Presumably these substance-less creatures had once had solid bodies, as I myself had had. Suppose that when they had been in their bodies that they had developed a dependence on alcohol that went beyond the physical. That became mental. Spiritual heaven. Then when they lost that body . . . they would be cut off for all eternity from the thing they could never stop craving.

Ritchie concluded from his experience that the Lord was showing him that those people who become addicted while on the earth and do not overcome their addiction during their lifetime will still have the addiction after they die. They still have the craving for the drugs, but they cannot satisfy their cravings because they no longer have a physical body, which is the only means by which addictive desires can be appeased.

Eadie also made observations on the relationship between our life on earth and what happens to us in the spirit world. She said that the types of lives we live, and the degree to which we place our thoughts and desires on earthly things versus spiritual things, affect what we do and where we go in the next life or even if we leave this earth at all.

They [her spirit guides] told me that it is important for us to acquire knowledge of the spirit while we are in the flesh. The more knowledge we acquire here, the further and faster we will progress there. Because of lack of knowledge or belief, some spirits are virtual prisoners of this earth. Some who die as atheists, or those who have bonded to the world through greed, bodily appetites, or other earthly commitments, find it difficult to move on, and they become earthbound. They often lack the faith and power to reach for, or in some cases to recognize, the energy and light that pulls us toward God. These spirits stay on the earth until they learn to accept the greater power around them and to let go of the world.

Ritchie learned that those who commit suicide fail to resolve whatever had been troubling them and discover that they are unable to escape the consequences of their act.

In one house a younger man followed an older one from room to room. "I'm sorry, Pa!" he kept saying. "I didn't know what it would do to Mama! I didn't understand."

But though I could hear him clearly, it was obvious that the man he was speaking to could not. The old man was carrying a tray into a room where an elderly woman sat in bed. "I'm sorry, Pa," the young man said again. "I'm sorry, Mama." Endlessly, over and over, to ears that could not hear.

In bafflement I turned to the Brightness [Being of Light] beside me. But though I felt His compassion flow like a torrent into the room before us, no understanding lightened my mind.

Several times we paused before similar scenes. A boy trailing a teenaged girl through the corridors of a school. "I'm sorry, Nancy!" A middle-aged woman begging a gray-haired man to forgive her.

"What are they so sorry for, Jesus?" I pleaded. "Why do they keep talking to people who can't hear them?"

Then from the light beside me came the thought: They are suicides, chained to every consequence of their act.

Joan Forman, in her near-death research, stated that

suicides on the far side of death find that they have solved nothing, and that the same set of problems which drove them to the act are still present. Since no matter how far the problems of a suicide appear to be rooted in his physical circumstances, the cause of the act is invariably an inability to deal psychologically with them, it is not surprising that the problems of the mind in life are still its problems after death. Death as an act, therefore, appears to impose no vital change upon the function of consciousness, apart from expanding it.

Nevertheless those who committed suicide and were permitted to return to their physical bodies discovered that they were still loved by the Being of Light and could be forgiven. But it was this life where they must face and resolve their problems.

In the late 1800s Rebecca Rutter Springer had an extensive NDE in which she visited the home that her brother had helped build for her. In this home she saw the walls were lined with rare and costly books. One of her first sensations was surprise at the sight of the books.

"Why have we books in heaven?"

"Why not?" asked my brother. "What strange ideas we mortals have of the pleasures and duties of this blessed life! We seem to think that the death of the body means an entire change to the soul. But this is not the case, by any means. We bring to this life the same tastes, the same desires, the same knowledge, we had before death. If these were not sufficiently pure and good to form a part of this life, then we ourselves may not enter. What would be the use of our ofttimes long lives, given to the pursuit of certain worthy and legitimate knowledge, if at death it all counts as nothing, and we begin this life on a wholly different line of thought and study? No, no; would that all could understand, as I have said before, that we are building for eternity during our earthly life! The purer the thoughts, the nobler the ambitions, the loftier the aspirations, the higher the rank we take among the hosts of heaven; the more earnestly we follow the studies and duties in our life of probation, the better fitted we shall be to carry them forward, on and on to completion and perfection here."

The foregoing accounts reveal that the kinds of lives we live while here on earth determine to a direct degree the kinds of lives we shall live on the other side. As discussed in chapter 10, there are multiple cities and locations within cities. Where individuals will dwell and the quality of their lives there is determined by their actions while on earth. Everyone knows who you are, what you have accomplished or failed to accomplish, and the effects your actions have had on the lives of others for good or ill. It appears that most individuals tend to seek out those who think, feel, and value the same things that they do. As everyone knows their most intimate thoughts, what they did in life, what they valued in life, they feel more comfortable with beings in the same condition as they are. In this regard—initially, at least—judgment seems to be more self-imposed than imposed by some tribunal.

Yet one individual during her life review experienced a type of judgment that left her excited and forever changed.

I will never be afraid of death. I want to experience the exhilaration of that judgment scene again, the feeling of God's love and compassion sweeping through me. It was awesome—in the true meaning of the word. As the review ended, I was given my judgment. I knew exactly how I stood, and I was very pleased with it and its fairness.

The spirit takes with it a perfect memory when he or she dies, which facilitates the singular experience that some NDErs encounter—that of a life review. In this review the person sees, senses, and experiences all of his or her mortal life again, sometimes down to the most minute detail, reliving it as if it were happening at that very moment. Emanuel Swedenborg argues that mankind will be judged out of their own memories and that everything anyone has ever done or thought becomes an integral part of that person's memory. His description of the life review was made in the 1700s.

There were people who denied crimes and disgraceful things they had committed in the world. So lest people believe them innocent, all things were uncovered and reviewed out of their memory, in sequence, from their earliest age to the end. Foremost were matters of adultery and whoredom.

There were some people who had taken others in by evil devices and who had stolen. Their wiles and thefts were recounted one after another—many of them things hardly anyone in the world had known other than the thieves themselves. They admitted them, too (since they were made clear as daylight), together with every thought, intent, pleasure, and fear which had then combined to agitate their spirits.

There were people who took bribes and made a profit out of judicial decisions. These people were examined from their memory in similar fashion, and from this source everything they had done from the beginning to the end of their tenure of office was reviewed. There were details about how much and what kind, about the time, about the state of their mind and intent, all cast together in their remembrance, now brought out into sight. . . .

There was one person who thought nothing of disparaging others. I heard his disparaging remarks repeated in their sequence, his defamations as well, in the actual words—whom they were about, whom they were addressed to. All these elements were set forth and presented together in wholly lifelike fashion; yet the details had been studiously covered up by him while he had lived in the world. . . .

In short, each evil spirit is shown clearly all his evil deeds, his crimes, thefts, deceits, and devices. These are brought out of his own memory and proven; there is no room left out for denial, since all the attendant circumstances are visible at once. . . .

Let no one then believe that there is anything a person has thought within himself or done in secret that remains hidden after death. Let him rather believe that each and everything will then be visible as in broad daylight.

This same phenomenon was experienced by George Ritchie during his NDE two hundred years later.

When I say He knew everything about me, this was simply an observable fact. For into that room along with His radiant presence—simultaneously, though in telling about it I have to describe them one by one—had also entered every single episode of my entire life. Everything that had ever happened to me was simply there, in full view, contemporary and current, all seemingly taking place at that moment.

Raymond Moody, in reflecting about the impact of the life review, observed:

In thinking about all this, it has occurred to me that a very common theme of near-death experiences is the feeling of being "exposed" in one way or another. From one point of view we human beings can be characterized as creatures who spend a great deal of time hiding behind various masks. We seek inner security through money or power; we pride ourselves on our social class, the degree of our education, the color of our bodies. . . . We adorn our bodies with clothes; we hide our innermost thoughts and certain of our deeds from the knowledge or sight of others.

However, in the moments around the time of death all such masks are necessarily dropped. Suddenly the person finds his every thought and deed portrayed in a three-dimensional, full-color panorama. If he meets other beings he reports that they know his every thought and vice versa.

This situation can be regarded as being most unpleasant indeed, and it is no wonder that quite frequently people may come back from this feeling that they need to make a change in their lives.

Everything we have ever thought or done is permanently stored in our memories. These memories come back vividly to the individual during the review. It would appear that the review (according to Moody) is not a final but a preliminary judgment, as the "Being of Light" who seems to be officiating does not in any way reject them. After seeing their lives, some individuals are given a second chance. Things that they have not yet done, but have committed to do, can yet be done. They may be given a chance to correct things they have done that hurt others in some way. The following account of a young man who was badly injured in an automobile accident and Howard Storm's account serve as fitting conclusions to this chapter.

The young man found himself in a very large room with other people when a being with a bright aura entered. His light completely engulfed him with a feeling of intense warmth and total love. The young man also had a total trust and an intense warmth and love toward this person that was unlike anything he ever had for anything or anybody.

The being then asked him, "Do you know where you are?"

He said, "Yes."

Then the being asked, "What is your decision?"

When the being said that the young man immediately had

a complete and clear knowledge of everything that had ever happened in his life, even the most minute things. He also knew that everybody in the room also knew these things. There were no secrets there, nothing could be hidden.

He realized that every person is sent to earth to experience things and to learn.

> For instance, to share more love, to be more loving toward one another. To discover that the most important thing is human relationships and love and not materialistic things.

He also discovered that everything a person does and thinks in life is recorded—including incidents we would consider very trivial. For instance, he realized for the first time the virtue of patience and that we must exercise patience with everyone since we will often be in need of patience from others.

Howard Storm also discovered that patient, true love and the so-called little things we do for others are what really matter. During his experience he was surrounded by brilliant beings.

> Next, they wanted to talk about my life. To my surprise my life played out before me, maybe six or eight feet in front of me, from beginning to end. The life review was very much in their control, and they showed me my life, but not from my point of view. I saw me in my life—and this whole thing was a lesson, even though I didn't know it at the time. They were trying to teach me something, but I didn't

know it was a teaching experience, because I didn't know that I would be coming back.

We just watched my life from the beginning to the end. Some things they slowed down on, and zoomed in on, and other things they went right through. My life was shown in a way that I had never thought of before. All the things that I had worked to achieve, the recognition that I had worked for, in elementary school, in high school, in college, and in my career, they meant nothing in this setting.

I could feel their feelings of sorrow and suffering, or joy, as my life's review unfolded. They didn't say that something was bad or good, but I could feel it. And I could sense all those things they were indifferent to. They didn't, for example, look down on my high school shot-put record. They just didn't feel anything towards it, nor towards other things which I had taken so much pride in.

What they responded to was how I had interacted with other people. That was the long and short of it. Unfortunately, most of my interactions with other people didn't measure up with how I should have interacted which was in a loving way.

Whenever I did react during my life in a loving way, they rejoiced. Most of the time I found that my interactions with other people had been manipulative. During my professional career, for example, I saw myself sitting in my office, playing the college professor, while a student came to me with a personal problem. I sat there looking compassionate, and patient, and loving, while inside I was bored to death. I would check my watch under my desk as I anxiously waited for the student to finish.

I got to go through all those kinds of experiences in the company of these magnificent beings. When I was a teenager my father's career put him into a high stress, twelve-hour-a-day job. Out of my resentment because of his neglect of me, when he came home from work, I would be cold and indifferent toward him. This made him angry, and it gave me a further excuse to feel hatred toward him. He and I fought, and my mother would get upset.

I got to see, when my sister had a bad night one night, how I went into her bedroom and put my arms around her. Not saying anything, I just lay there with my arms around her. As it turned out that experience was one of the biggest triumphs of my life.

The entire life's review would have been emotionally destructive, and would have left me a psychotic person, if it hadn't been for the fact that my friend, and my friend's friends, were loving me during the unfolding of my life. I could feel that love. Every time I got a little upset they turned the life's review off for a while, and they just loved me. Their love was tangible. You could feel it on your body, you could feel it inside of you; their love went right through you.

Summary

The implication of NDE research is that we lived as full-grown spirits in a pre-earth life in another realm before earth life. Among our pre-earth life activities were making commitments to do specific things on earth, associating with individuals and living in various locations in the pre-earth life while waiting to come to earth.

The communication between parents and their soon-to-be children helps illustrate the relationship between pre-earth life and earth life. Many of these parents realized they knew their children as individuals they had known, loved, and committed themselves to help before earth life.

Earth life is apparently a necessary experience for spirit beings, a time when individuals are to accomplish their specific work and to gain knowledge and experience.

At death, one's personality continues relatively unaltered from earth life. The types of lives people live will determine what they will do and where they go in the next life. Everything we do, say, and think is stored as part of our unique identity that accompanies us into the next life.

Thus, there is continuous life from one stage to the next, and the activities of one are connected to the other and dependent on the earlier stage, with the pre-earth life coming first, followed by earth life, which is then followed by a post-earth life.

CHAPTER 16

Closing Comments

Near-death research has shed new understanding on this earthly life and its meaning and purpose as well as on the previous life and the life to come. In essence, this body of scientific data provides what appears to be newly discovered, or possibly rediscovered, truth that suggests life did not begin at mortal birth, nor does it end at mortal death, also that human development and progress did not begin at birth and will not end at death.

Here is Jean's final near-death experience witness:

> I know that there was life before this life, and I know that there is life after death. I also know that this life is a testing period, kind of a school. And that the people on both sides—in the life prior to this life, and those that are living in the spirit world after having died—are concerned about us and care about us. I think that the ones in the spirit world,

after death, have more contact with us than those who have not yet been born.

I know that our deceased relatives are alive. I believe that when we pray and invite them to be with us they are allowed to come, if they are worthy. In order for them to visit us we must invite them, otherwise they can't come. Finally, I know that the spirit world is so peaceful and calm, and we are all going to be so happy to be there, that if we knew what it was like . . . well, there is no way we would want to stay on earth.

With this increased understanding, people should desire to live better lives as well as appreciate death for what it really is—a transition to another world.

Will people listen and use this understanding of life and its "purposes" to change their lives? Recent studies suggest that exposure to information about the NDE such as the information contained in this book can bring about substantial changes in beliefs about NDEs, life after death, and God, as well as reduce fear of death and increase one's level of spirituality. If they do so, surely many of society's problems will solve themselves. Further upheaval and destruction in the world would stop. Humanity would eventually be characterized by love and peace.

However, and just as important, is the fact that living a better life will improve our situation after death. Betty Eadie's guides in the otherworld told her that after death people go to the level to which their spirit has grown. Eadie understood, as did Emanuel Swedenborg, George Ritchie, Howard Storm, and others, that there are many levels of development or communities and we will always go to the level or community where we are most comfortable.

Their testimony is also clear that in death we do not suddenly change, we will not escape our problems, and that our thoughts and desires go with us for good or ill. We should be less concerned about how others may react to us, than how our lives and actions impact on others.

Although the history of humankind argues against a dramatic change in how societies function, there have been temporary periods of considerable peace on the earth. In those periods, men and women seem to have recognized the importance of the spiritual aspects of existence and conformed to the universal laws that govern the earth. So there still remains hope that people will follow Melvin Morse's admonition to "learn what you can about life from these brushes with death, even if they are the experiences of other people." If we do not, peace may come only through some future calamity upon the earth that has been foreseen in the prophetic visions of some near-death experiencers. On a personal level, we will hinder, stunt, or even reverse our growth and development if we do not listen, hear what NDErs have to say, and act accordingly.

Near-death experiences and the visions of the dying relating to the next world reveal that all life has meaning, that we all have some purpose for being on earth, and that death does not destroy us or our relationships.

However, most important in life and death is love. If there is a single message that characterizes the near-death experience, it is love. It fills the next world and engulfs those who go there and experience it. The NDE researcher Arvin S. Gibson notes, as have many other researchers, that upon returning to this life, NDErs feel the most important message they bring back with them is that we should love everybody with unconditional love. This message was given to a son by a father who received permission to visit him.

Dave had witnessed much death and carnage during his experience as an ambulance driver during the Second World War. He survived war only to lose his father to encephalitis resulting from a mosquito bite. His father's death seemed so senseless and Dave was overwhelmed by his loss. He was grieving deeply when the following occurred.

> I was stretched on my bed, dog-tired from the day's rigorous, non-stop training activities and had closed my eyes, expecting to immediately drop off to sleep. Suddenly I saw the image of my dad in my mind—as real and alive as though he was actually in the room. It was like a dream, only I was still awake.
>
> "Hyuh, Dave," he said, smiling warmly, "I thought I'd drop in on you just to let you know I am still alive."
>
> He was deeply tanned, tall, lean and handsome in one of his usual graceful, brown suits; his silver-blue eyes were full of light. He looked wonderful.
>
> "My God—Dad!" I exclaimed. "Is it really you?"
>
> He smiled, amused. "Yes, it's me all right, Dave. You thought I died back last April, didn't you? Well, in the words of Mark Twain, the reports of my death are highly exaggerated."
>
> "Obviously Mark Twain was right about you," I said. "You really look terrific."

He sat down on the edge of my bed. "Well, Dave, I sure got a surprise after the doctors declared I was dead. I'd always thought death meant the end of one's life." There was a twinkle in his eyes. "You know you people on earth are a lot deader than we are. . . . I now know that there's a Higher Power and that God and Love are one and the same and these are the only things that matter in the whole damned universe. Most of what we think is important when we're on earth—getting ahead, being successful, making it big in business or politics or in a profession, making a lot of money, achieving high rank—are just chaff that the wind blows away. What really counts is what you did for others—how much you loved beyond yourself— how much you really loved and how well!

"Dave, I came back for just one very particular reason—to stop you from grieving about my so-called 'death.' I wasn't sure whether I'd be able to get through to you—but now that you see how alive I am, you can understand how pointless it is to grieve—it really makes it harder for us to do what we're meant to do. . . . Just remember from now on that we're not only still alive but more alive than we ever were before—so when you think about me, I want you to be happy for me, not mournful."

This man's message to his son was that he is alive, that he now knows what is really important—unconditional love. He also wanted his son to know that his work in the spirit world was being affected by his son's grief. Death is not the end of life, just the opposite. It is the beginning of real life.

Teresa also experienced this universal love during her NDE:

> The key to growth in the future is to love ourselves and to extend that love to others. The interconnectedness of all living beings, and the love we feel for all life, are gifts from God. The Lord made it possible for us to love as we should, but we often deny ourselves that privilege. When we grieve, we should know that we are grieving tears of precious love—a love for the connectedness of all humans. . . .
>
> In my life's review I understood that my life was lived, not just for me, but for others that I interact with. We are all connected in God's plan. We, and every other living thing, affect everything else.

Those who read these experiences from persons who have experienced death and returned to life to share their newfound knowledge of an eternal journey beyond death, will understand the true purpose of life and meaning of death.

Sources for Quoted Material
(by order of appearance)

CHAPTER 1: Introduction

Melvin Morse and Paul Perry, *Transformed by the Light* (New York: Villard Books, 1992), p. 77.

CHAPTER 2: The Reality of the Near-Death Experience

Ian Wilson, *The After Death Experience—The Physics of the Non-Physical* (New York: William Morrow & Company, Inc., 1987), pp. 132–133.

Raymond A. Moody Jr. and Paul Perry, *The Light Beyond* (New York: Bantam Books, Inc., 1988), p. 154.

Kenneth Ring, "Prophetic Visions in 1998: A Critical Reappraisal," *Journal of Near-Death Studies* (Vol. 7, No. I, Fall 1988), p. 5.

George Gallup Jr. and William Proctor, *Adventures in Immortality* (New York: McGraw-Hill, 1982).

Duane S. Crowther, *Life Everlasting* (Salt Lake City, Utah: Bookcraft, Inc., 1967), pp. 145–146.

CHAPTER 3: *Pre-Earth Life and Its Purposes*

Betty J. Eadie and Curtis Taylor, *Embraced by the Light* (Placerville, California: Gold Leaf Press, 1992), p. 44.

Herman Stulz, Diary: 1896–1959 (Salt Lake City, Utah: Unpublished, Historical Archives of the Church of Jesus Christ of Latter-day Saints), pp. 6–7.

Arvin S. Gibson, *Echoes from Eternity: New Near-Death Experiences Examined* (Bountiful, Utah: Horizon Publishers, 1993), pp. 70–71.

Ibid., p. 124.

Crowther, *Life Everlasting*, p. 39.

Sarah Hinze, *Life Before Life* (Springville, Utah: Cedar Fort, Inc., 1993), pp. 115–116. (This book was revised and published again by Pocket Books in 1997 under the title *Coming From the Light: Spiritual Accounts of the Life Before Life.*)

Arvin S. Gibson, *Glimpses of Eternity* (Bountiful, Utah: Horizon Publishers, 1992), pp. 87–88.

Hinze, *Life Before Life*, p. 79.

Howard Mickel, *The Near-Death Experience* (Wichita, Kansas: Theta Project, 1985), p. 31.

Melvin Morse and Paul Perry, *Closer to the Light* (New York: Villard Books, 1990), p. 123.

Gibson, *Glimpses of Eternity*, p. 171.

Hinze, *Life Before Life*, pp. 94–97.

Lee Nelson, *Beyond the Veil*, Volume I (Orem, Utah: Cedar Fort, Inc., 1988), pp. 37–39.

Ibid., pp. 107–109.

Eadie and Taylor, *Embraced by the Light*, pp. 89–90.

Ibid., pp. 92–93.

Ibid., p. 68.

Ibid., p. 95.

Ibid., p. 42.

CHAPTER 4: *Earth Life and Its Purposes*

Michele R. Sorensen and David R. Willmore, *The Journey Beyond Life*, Volume I (Orem, Utah: Family Affair Books, 1988), pp. 89–91.

Eadie and Taylor, *Embraced by the Light*, pp. 67 and 71.

Ibid., p. 58.

Ibid., p. 59.

Ranelle Wallace and Curtis Taylor, *The Burning Within* (Carson City, Nevada: Gold Leaf Press, 1994), p. 105.

Ibid., p. 116.

Brad Steiger, *One with the Light* (New York: Penguin Books, 1994), p. 94.

Ibid., p. 142.

Gibson, *Echoes from Eternity*, p. 195.

Moody and Perry, *The Light Beyond*, p. 33.

Lee Nelson, *Beyond the Veil*, Volume II (Orem, Utah: Cedar Fort, Inc., 1989), p. 47.

Ibid., p. 153.

Eadie and Taylor, *Embraced by the Light*, pp. 50–51.

Ibid., p. 101.

Gibson, *Glimpses of Eternity*, pp. 188–190.

Gibson, *Echoes from Eternity*, p. 71.

Kenneth Ring, *Heading Toward Omega* (New York: William Morrow and Company, Inc., 1985), p. 70.

Morse and Perry, *Transformed by the Light*, p. 218.

Gibson, *Echoes from Eternity*, p. 126.

Ibid., p. 145.

Ibid., p. 172.

Melvin S. Tagg, "The Life of Edward James Wood," Unpublished Master's Thesis, College of Religious Instruction, Brigham Young University, Provo, Utah, 1959, pp. 88–89.

Raymond A. Moody Jr., *Life after Life* (New York: Bantam Books, Inc., 1975), p. 93.

Gallup and Proctor, *Adventures in Immortality*, p. 129.

Moody and Perry, *The Light Beyond*, p. 127.

Joseph Heinerman, *Spirit World Manifestations* (Salt Lake City, Utah: Magazine Printing and Publishing, 1978), p. 270.

Morse and Perry, *Closer to the Light*, p. 155.

Sorensen and Willmore, *The Journey Beyond Life*, Volume I, p. 133.

Ibid., p. 174.

Michael B. Sabom and Sarah Kreutiziger, "The Experience of Near-Death," *Death Education* (Volume 1, 1977), p. 200.

D. Scott Rogo, *The Return from Silence: A Study of Near-Death Experience* (The Aquarian Press, 1989), p. 222.

Margot Grey, *Return from Death: An Exploration of the Near-Death Experience* (New York: Arkana, 1985), pp. 79–80.

Gibson, *Echoes from Eternity*, p. 177.

Nelson, *Beyond the Veil*, Volume II, p. 51.

Robert Crookall, *What Happens When You Die* (Gerrards Cross: Colin Smythe, 1978), p. 19.

Alfred Smedley, *Some Reminiscences* (London: Office of Light, 1900), pp. 52–53.

Nelson, *Beyond the Veil,* Volume II, p. 12.

Ibid., p. 21.

Gibson, *Glimpses of Eternity,* p. 147.

Steiger, *One with the Light,* p. 131.

Eadie and Taylor, *Embraced by the Light,* p. 116.

Ring, *Heading Toward Omega,* p. 197.

Ibid., p. 198.

CHAPTER 5: *The Death Transition*

Nelson, *Beyond the Veil,* Volume I, p. 67.

———, *Beyond the Veil,* Volume III (Orem, Utah: Cedar Fort, Inc., 1989), p. 146.

Eadie and Taylor, *Embraced by the Light,* p. 83.

Sorensen and Willmore, *The Journey Beyond Life,* Volume I, pp. 36–37.

Karlis Osis and Erlendur Haraldsson, *At the Hour of Death* (New York: Avon Books, 1977), p. 4.

Gallup and Proctor, *Adventures in Immortality,* pp. 13–14.

Gibson, *Glimpses of Eternity,* p. 106.

Nelson, *Beyond the Veil,* Volume III, p. 56.

Gibson, *Glimpses of Eternity,* p. 122.

Ibid., p. 116

Morse and Perry, *Transformed by the Light,* p. 156.

Crowther, *Life Everlasting,* p. 8.

Moody, *Life After Life*, p. 29.

Ibid., p. 29.

Sorensen and Willmore, *The Journey Beyond Life*, Volume I, p. 73.

Eadie and Taylor, *Embraced by the Light*, pp. 83–84.

Nelson, *Beyond the Veil*, Volume II, p. 146.

CHAPTER 6: Death: Crossing into the World of Light

Sorensen and Willmore, *The Journey Beyond Life*, Volume I, p. 90.

Joy Snell, *The Ministry of Angels* (New York: Citadel Press, 1918), pp. 38–39.

Catherine Marshall, *To Live Again* (New York: Avon Books, 1957), pp. 199–200.

R. William Barrett, *Death-Bed Visions* (London: Psychic Book Club, 1926), p. 12.

Anonymous, personal communication with H. A. Widdison, 1993.

Gordan Lindsay (ed.), *Scenes Beyond the Grave* (Dallas, Texas: Christ for the Nations, 1974), pp. 21–22.

John Myers, *Voices from the Edge of Eternity* (Old Tappan, N.J.: Spire Books, 1968), p. 161.

Morse and Perry, *Closer to the Light*, p. 7.

Gibson, *Glimpses of Eternity*, p. 53.

James H. Hyslop, *Psychical Research and the Resurrection* (Boston: Small, Maynard and Company, 1908), p. 85.

William Dudley Pelley, "Seven Minutes in Eternity," *Improvement Era* (vol. 32, June 1929), pp. 622–624.

Alfred Smedley, *Some Reminiscences* (London: British Lyceum Union, 1900), pp. 50–51.

J. Arthur Hill, *Man Is Spirit* (New York: Cassell and Company, Ltd., 1918), p. 98.

Gibson, *Echoes from Eternity*, p. 81.

Snell, *The Ministry of Angels*, pp. 41–43.

Gibson, *Glimpses of Eternity*, pp. 13–14.

CHAPTER 7: *The Nature of the Spirit Body*

Arvin S. Gibson, *Theresa's Story* (Bountiful, Utah: By the author, 1994), p. 3.

Ibid., pp. 3–4.

George G. Ritchie and Elizabeth Sherrill, *Return from Tomorrow* (Waco, Texas: Chosen Books, 1978), p. 48.

Gibson, *Echoes from Eternity*, p. 279.

Herman Stulz, Diary: 1896–1959, pp. 6–8.

Craig R. Lundahl, "Near-Death Experiences of Mormons," in Craig R. Lundahl (comp.), *A Collection of Near Death Research Readings* (Chicago: Nelson-Hall, Inc., 1982), pp. 170–171.

Nelson, *Beyond the Veil*, Volume III, p. 132.

Gibson, *Theresa's Story*, p. 9.

———, *Echoes from Eternity*, p. 122.

Margot Grey, *Return from Death*, p. 53.

Robert Crookall, *More Astral Projections* (London: Aquarian Press, 1964), p. 102.

George G. Ritchie, *My Life After Dying* (Norfolk, Va.: Hampton Roads Publishing Company, 1991), p. 24.

Marvin Ford, *On the Other Side* (Plainfield, N.J.: Logos International, 1978), p. 42.

Michael B. Sabom, *Recollections of Death* (New York: Harper & Row, 1982), p. 48.

Gibson, *Theresa's Story*, p. 5.

Maurice Rawlings, *Beyond Death's Door* (Nashville, Tenn.: Thomas Nelson, 1978), p. 80.

Gallup and Proctor, *Adventures in Immortality*, p. 14.

Betty Malz, *My Glimpse of Eternity* (Old Tappan, N.J.: Spire Books, 1977), p. 84.

Gibson, *Glimpses of Eternity*, p. 164.

Echoes from Eternity, pp. 72–73.

Archie Matson, *Afterlife: Reports from the Threshold of Death* (New York: Harper & Row, 1975), p. 35.

Gibson, *Glimpses of Eternity*, p. 122.

Ibid., p. 148.

Ibid., p 145–146.

Ibid., p. 45.

"Susan Burt," *IANDS of Utah* newsletter (September/October 1994), p. 2.

Grey, *Return from Death*, p. 49.

John Oxenham and Erica Oxenham, *Out of the Body* (New York: Longmans, Green and Company, 1941), pp. 3–4.

Joseph Heinerman, *Guardian Angels* (Salt Lake City, Utah: Joseph Lyon & Associates, 1985), p. 115.

David P. Wheeler, *Journey to the Other Side* (New York: Ace Books, 1977), p. 102.

Oxenham and Oxenham, *Out of the Body*, pp. 13–16.

Gibson, *Echoes from Eternity*, p. 122.

William J. Serdahely, "Loving Help from the Other Side," *Journal of Near-Death Studies* (vol. 10, No. 3, Spring 1992), p. 174.

Grey, *Return from Death*, p. 79.

Ford, *On the Other Side*, p. 84.

Rawlings, *Beyond Death's Door*, p. 102.

Morse and Perry, *Transformed by the Light*, p. 53.

Gibson, *Echoes from Eternity*, pp. 291–292.

Ritchie, *My Life After Dying*, p. 24.

Richard F. Eby, *Caught up into Paradise* (Old Tappan, N.J.: Fleming H. Revell, 1971), p. 203.

CHAPTER 8: *The Location of the Afterlife*

S. H. Dryden, *Daisy Dryden: A Memoir* (Boston: Colonial Press, 1909), pp. 37–39, 43–44, and 46–47.

Gibson, *Echoes from Eternity*, p. 210.

Louis Tucker, *Clerical Errors* (New York: Harper & Row, 1943), p. 223.

Cherie Sutherland, *Life After Near-Death Experiences* (Sydney: Bantam Books, 1992), p. 8.

Morse and Perry, *Transformed by the Light*, p. 8.

Raymond A. Moody Jr., *Reflections on Life After Life* (New York: Bantam, 1977), pp. 34–35.

C. D. DeMorgan, *From Matter to Spirit* (London: Longman, Green, Longman, Roberts & Green, 1863), p. 179.

Sorensen and Willmore, *The Journey Beyond Life*, Volume I, p. 91.

Eadie and Taylor, *Embraced by the Light*, p. 83.

Nelson, *Beyond the Veil*, Volume II, p. 140.

Oxenham and Oxenham, *Out of the Body*, pp. 57–58.

Ford, *On the Other Side*, p. 167.

Dryden, *Daisy Dryden*, pp. 44–45.

Oxenham and Oxenham, *Out of the Body*, pp. 79–80.

CHAPTER 9: *Approaching the City of Light*

Grey, *Return from Death*, p. 50.

Oxenham and Oxenham, *Out of the Body*, pp. 3–4.

Snell, *The Ministry of Angels*, p. 165.

S. J. Muldoon and H. Carrington, *The Phenomena of Astral Projection* (New York: Samuel Weiger, 1974), p. 76.

William J. Serdahely, "A Pediatric Near-Death Experience," *Omega* (Vol. 20, 1989–1990), p. 59.

David R. Wheeler, *Journey to the Other Side* (New York: Ace Books, 1977), p. 104.

Heinerman, *Guardian Angels*, p. 116.

Grey, *Return from Death*, p. 50.

Snell, *The Ministry of Angels*, p. 93.

Ford, *On the Other Side*, p. 5.

Richard E. Eby, *Caught up into Paradise*, pp. 206–207.

Sorensen and Willmore, *The Journey Beyond Life*, Volume I, p. 111.

Oxenham and Oxenham, *Out of the Body*, p. 14.

Nelson, *Beyond the Veil*, Volumn I, p. 123.

Stulz, Diary: 1896–1959.

Tucker, *Clerical Errors*, p. 222.

Grey, *Return from Death*, p. 49.

Nelson, *Beyond the Veil*, Volume I, pp. 60–61.

William Dudley Pelley, "Seven Minutes in Eternity," *Improvement Era* (vol. 32, June 1929), pp. 623–624.

Moody, *Reflections on Life After Life*, p. 17.

CHAPTER 10: The City of Light

Gibson, *Glimpses of Eternity*, p. 13.

Rawlings, *Beyond Death's Door*, p. 78.

Ritchie and Sherrill, *Return from Tomorrow*, p. 72.

Ring, *Heading Toward Omega*, p. 72.

Eadie and Taylor, *Embraced by the Light*, pp. 78–79.

Nelson, *Beyond the Veil*, Volume III, p. 99.

Sylvain Muldoon, *The Case for Astral Projection* (Chicago, Ill.: Aries Press, 1936), p. 142.

Eadie and Taylor, *Embraced by the Light*, p. 108.

Jean-Baptiste Delacour, *Glimpses of the Beyond* (New York: Delacorte Press, 1978), p. 59.

Sorensen and Willmore, *The Journey Beyond Life*, Volume I, p. 111.

Nelson, *Beyond the Veil*, Volume II, p. 51.

Gibson, *Glimpses of Eternity*, pp. 176–177.

Ritchie, *My Life After Dying*, pp. 27–28.

Ritchie and Sherrill, *Return from Tomorrow*, pp. 68–72.

Gibson, *Glimpses of Eternity*, p. 177.

Ford, *The Life Beyond Death*, p. 203.

Nelson, *Beyond the Veil*, Volume I, pp. 21–22.

Heinerman, *Guardian Angels*, pp. 130–131.

Ibid., p. 104.

Ibid., p. 104.

John Powell, Journal of John Powell (unpublished manuscript), pp. 76–78.

Raymond Bayless, *The Other Side of Death* (New Hyde Park, N.Y.: University Books, 1971), p. 101.

Herr Pettersson, "In the World of Spirits," *Millennial Star* (Vol. 89, No. 4, Jan. 4, 1917), pp. 1–7.

CHAPTER 11: *Life in the City of Light*

Nelson, *Beyond the Veil,* Volume I, p. 101.

Grey, *Return from Death*, p. 52.

Ford, *The Life Beyond Death*, p. 203.

Sorensen and Willmore, *The Journey Beyond Life*, Volume I, pp. 110–111.

LeRoi Snow, "Raised from the Dead," Improvement Era (Vol. 32, No. 12, October 1929), p. 977.

Ritchie and Sherrill, *Return from Tomorrow*, p. 69.

Gibson, *Echoes from Eternity*, p. 103.

Muldoon and Carrington, *The Phenomena of Astral Projection*, p. 138.

Moody and Perry, *The Light Beyond* p. 111.

Nelson, *Beyond the Veil,* Volume II, pp. 16–18.

————, *Beyond the Veil,* Volume I, pp. 22–23.

Grey, *Return from Death*, pp. 54–55.

Sorensen and Willmore, *The Journey Beyond Life,* Volume I, p. 111.

Heinerman, *Guardian Angels*, p. 132.

Crowther, *Life Everlasting*, pp. 101–102.

Gibson, *Echoes from Eternity*, pp. 121–122.

Ibid., p. 173.

Nelson, *Beyond the Veil*, Volume I, p. 63.
Eadie and Taylor, *Embraced by the Light*, p. 75.
Grey, *Return from Death*, p. 79.
Gibson, *Glimpses of Eternity*, p. 53.
Eadie and Taylor, *Embraced by the Light*, pp. 31–32.
Gibson, *Echoes from Eternity*, p. 103.
————, *Glimpses of Eternity*, p. 171.
Tucker, *Clerical Errors*, p. 223.
Kenneth Ring, "Amazing Grace," *Journal of Near Death Studies* (Vol. 10, No. 1, Fall 1991), p. 30.

CHAPTER 12: *The Purposes of Post-Earth Life*

Steiger, *One with the Light*, pp. 88–89.
Crowther, *Life Everlasting*, p. 205.
Oxenham and Oxenham, *Out of the Body*, p. 45.
Ritchie, *My Life after Dying*, p. 25.
Sorensen and Willmore, *The Journey Beyond Life*, p. 168.
N. B. Lundwall, *The Vision* (Salt Lake City, Utah: Bookcraft, n.d.), p. 72.

CHAPTER 13: *Angels*

Morse and Perry, *Transformed by the Light*, p. xi.
Gibson, *Glimpses of Eternity*, pp. 52–53.
Moody and Perry, *The Light Beyond*, pp. 58–59.
Dryden, *Daisy Dryden*.

Kenneth Ring, "Frequency and Stages of the Protypic Near-Death Experience," in Craig R. Lundahl (comp.), *A Collection of Near-Death Research Readings* (Chicago: Nelson Hall, 1982), p. 143.

Ford, *On the Other Side*, p. 41.

Ring, "Amazing Grace," p. 15.

Raymond Bayless, *The Other Side of Death*, p. 100.

Michael B. Sabom and Sarah Kreutziger, "The Experience of Near-Death," *Death Education*, p. 200.

C. W. Leadbeater, *Invisible Helpers* (London: The Theosophical Book Company, 1901), pp. 12–13.

Ibid., p. 15.

Nelson, *Beyond the Veil*, pp. 31–32.

Stokes, *Modern Miracles*, pp. 53–54.

John Myers, *Voices from the Edge of Eternity*, p. 161.

John Petterson, "Was Dead and Came Back to Life Again," *Millennial Star* (Vol. 68, July 1929), p. 699.

Heinerman, *Guardian Angels*, p. 121.

Stulz, Diary: 1896–1959.

Gibson, *Echoes from Eternity*, pp. 158–159.

Barrett, *Death-Bed Visions*, p. 75.

DeMorgan, *From Matter to Spirit*, p. 185.

Barrett, *Death-Bed Visions*, p. 87.

Gibson, *Glimpses of Eternity*, pp. 104–105.

Ring, "Amazing Grace," p. 30.

James H. Hyslop, "Visions of the Dying," *Journal of the American Society for Psychical Research* (Vol. 10, 1918), pp. 619–620.

James Beck, Diary (Salt Lake City, Utah: Unpublished, Historical Society Archives of the Church of Jesus Christ of Latter-day Saints, n.d.).

Arvin S. Gibson, Howard Storm: Questions and Answer Period (Bountiful, Utah: Transcription from an audiotape, n.d.), p. 4.

CHAPTER 14: The Realm of Bewildered Spirits

Arvin S. Gibson, "Commentary on 'Frightening Near-Death Experiences,'" Journal of Near-Death Studies (Vol. 15, Number 2, Winter 1996), pp. 141–148.
Grey, Return from Death, p. 64.
Ibid., pp. 68–69.
Ibid., p. 69.
Gibson, Glimpses of Eternity, p. 254.
Don Brubaker, Absent from the Body, pp. 77, 80–82, 86, 99, 103–104.
Gibson, Echoes from Eternity, pp. 254–255.
Heinerman, Guardian Angels, pp. 150–151.
Crowther, Life Everlasting, pp. 155–156.
Bayless, The Other Side of Death, p. 101.
Moody, Reflections on Life After Life, p. 18.

CHAPTER 15: The Connection between Pre-Earth Life, Earth Life, and Post-Earth Life

Eadie and Taylor, Embraced by the Light, p. 96.
Hinze, Life before Life, p. 25.
Ibid., pp. 85–86.
Ibid., pp. 144–145.

Carol Jeanne Ehlers and Vicki Jo Robinson, *Opening the Windows of Heaven* (Salt Lake City, Utah: Hawkes Publishing, 1987), pp. 37–38.

Hinze, *Life Before Life*, pp. 6–7.

Ibid., p. 108.

Ibid., p. 37.

Ibid., p. 117.

Ibid., p. 49.

P. M. H. Atwater, *Beyond the Light* (New York: Birch Lane Press, 1994), p. 177.

Grey, *Return from Death*, p. 50.

Glen O. Gabbard and Stuart W. Twemlow, *With the Eyes of the Mind* (New York: Praeger Publishers, 1984), p. 127.

Gibson, *Theresa's Story*, p. 13

Sorensen and Willmore, *The Journey Beyond Life*, Volume I, p. 92.

Heinerman, *Guardian Angels*, p. 153.

Ritchie and Sherrill, *Return from Tomorrow*, pp. 59–61.

Eadie and Taylor, *Embraced by the Light*, p. 84.

Ritchie and Sherrill, *Return from Tomorrow*, pp. 58–59.

Joan Forman, *The Golden Shore* (London: Futura Book, 1988), p. 69.

Rebecca Rutter Springer, *My Dream of Heaven* (Midway, Utah: M.A.P., n.d.), pp. 23–24.

Sorensen and Willmore, *The Journey Beyond Life*, Volume I, p. 92.

Emanuel Swedenborg, *Heaven and Hell*, translated by George F. Dole (New York: Swedenborg Foundation, 1990), pp. 462b–463.

Ritchie and Sherrill, *Return from Tomorrow*, pp. 49–50.

Moody, *Reflections on Life After Life*, pp. 33–35.

Arvin S. Gibson, *Journeys Beyond Life* (Bountiful, Utah: Horizon Publishers, 1994), pp. 218–220.

CHAPTER 16: Closing Comments

Gibson, *Glimpses of Eternity*, p. 311.
David Hyatt, *Your Life & Love Beyond Death*, pp. 162–166.
Gibson, *Theresa's Story*, pp. 15–16.

About the Authors

Craig R. Lundahl, Ph.D., is one of the original near-death researchers in the field of near-death studies, beginning his studies on the subject in 1977. He is best known for his work that brought attention to Mormon near-death experiences. He also taught the first course offered exclusively on the near-death experience at a university in the United States. He has authored one book and authored and coauthored (with Harold A. Widdison) many professional articles on the near-death experience. He has presented his work at national and international conferences. He is Professor Emeritus of Sociology and Business Administration and Chair Emeritus of the Department of Social Sciences at Western New Mexico University and serves as Senior Professor at Senior University in Richmond, British Columbia, Canada. In the past he has served in various educational and administrative positions in higher education. He is a member of the International Association of Near-Death Studies (IANDS). Dr. Lundahl received his doctorate in sociology from Utah State University and has done postdoctoral work at Harvard University and the University of Michigan. He has a forthcoming book titled *Principles of Life: The Nature of Humanity and America's Decline.*

Harold A. Widdison, Ph.D., is a pioneer in the field of death education. He taught one of the first courses on death, grief, and bereavement in 1972. Since 1972 he has presented professional workshops, papers, and research at national and international conferences on death and near-death experiences. His interest in near-death experiences is both professional and personal. He served on the board of the Northern Arizona Regional Medical Center and presently serves on the board of directors for the Hozhoni Foundation for the Handicapped and as Professor of Sociology at Northern Arizona University. He is a member of the International Association of Near-Death Studies (IANDS). Dr. Widdison has a doctorate in medical sociology from Case Western Reserve University. He has a forthcoming book titled *Listen to the Children: What Children Can Teach Us about Life and Death.*

Index

291